P-M Analysis

P-M Analysis

An Advanced Step in TPM Implementation

Kunio Shirose

Yoshifumi Kimura

Mitsugu Kaneda

Productivity Press • *New York*

Originally published as *PM Bunseki*, © 1990 by the Japan Institute of Plant Maintenance.

English translation © 1995 by Productivity Press, a division of Kraus Productivity Organization, Ltd. Translated by Andrew P. Dillon and Bruce Talbot.

Productivity Press
444 Park Avenue South, Suite 604
New York, NY 10016
United States of America
Telephone: 212-686-5900
Telefax: 212-686-5411
E-mail: info@productivitypress.com

Cover and page design by William Stanton
Composition and page finishing by Frank Loose Design
Illustrations by Laser Words, Productivity Press (India) Private Ltd., and Frank Loose Design

Library of Congress Cataloging-in-Publication Data

Shirose, Kunio.
    [PM bunseki. English]
    P-M analysis : an advanced step in TPM implementation / Kunio Shirose, Yoshifumi Kimura,
and Mitsugu Kaneda.
        p.   cm.
    Includes index.
    ISBN 1-56327-312-8
    1. Production management. 2. Quality control. I. Kimura, Yoshifumi. II. Kaneda, Mitsugu.
III. Title.
TS155.S48513 1995
94-47031   658.5--dc20
                                                                          CIP

Contents

Steps 1 Through 4 Illustrated
P-M Analysis—The Full Cause-and-Effect Chain

Publisher's Message

In his book, *TPM for Workshop Leaders,* author Kunio Shirose defined TPM as "a set of activities for restoring equipment to its optimal conditions and changing the work environment to maintain those conditions." His nutshell definition highlights the principal shopfloor activities pursued in a TPM program: focused equipment or process improvement to reduce losses and collaborative maintenance carried out by production workers and skilled tradespeople. Both types of activity are critical to the success of a TPM program. But although preventive and autonomous (operator) maintenance are practiced in many American manufacturing environments today, programs for systematic equipment improvement that go beyond the scope of restoration and repair are usually found only in more advanced TPM implementations.

This book may help correct that imbalance. In *P-M Analysis,* TPM experts Kunio Shirose, Yoshifumi Kimura, and Mitsugu Kaneda detail a comprehensive 8-step method that has successfully eliminated chronic equipment-related problems in many PM Prize-winning companies. Chronic loss includes the final 1 to 5 percent of problems that must be solved to achieve a zero defect/zero failure environment. Chronic quality defects, for example, are especially difficult to eradicate, because they often have multiple, interrelated causes that vary with every occurrence. Common improvement strategies like cause-and-effect analysis and Pareto analysis are typically ineffective in dealing with such complex problems.

P-M ("P-dash-M") analysis was developed especially to overcome the weaknesses of traditional methods. For example, brainstorming and factor analysis are replaced by a rigorous analytical approach that identifies all potential causal factors. And, surprisingly, the accepted principle of prioritization is suspended at key points to ensure that all factors are addressed. Individual P-M analysis projects are conducted on a priority basis, but for each defect phenomenon or failure studied, all possible causal factors are identified, and every factor exhibiting abnormal conditions is investigated and corrected—regardless of the suspected degree of contribution.

Equipment improvement projects yield unsatisfactory results for a variety of reasons. Sometimes team members have not defined the abnormal occurrence with sufficient specificity, so their countermeasures miss the mark. In other cases, team members have inadequate knowledge of equipment structures and operating principles, so their factor analysis is incomplete. Through P-M analysis, however, teams develop an intimate understanding of their equipment. Its skill-building process helps team members improve their technological know-how and confidence as they develop solutions to persistent problems. The first 4 steps of this 8-step program help teams isolate and understand the root causes of defects and failures within main equipment mechanisms and peripheral systems. The final 4 steps provide a systematic approach for effectively controlling those causes.

A preliminary step in P-M analysis especially contributes to its rigor and skill-building: *physical analysis*—a way of thinking about how defects and failures are generated. Teams look at the physical principles involved and quantify the changes in the relationship between the equipment mechanisms and product or parts involved. When a proper physical analysis is carried out, teams are far less likely to overlook important factors or to waste time pursuing unrelated ones. Although not a cure-all, P-M analysis properly implemented has reduced chronic losses to zero and raised technological expertise in many manufacturing environments.

P-M analysis is probably not for environments struggling to counteract the effects of accelerated deterioration.[1] Rather, it is an essential tool for TPM improvement teams with some previous experience reducing equipment-related loss—teams who are primed to overcome the remaining obstacles to a zero loss environment. Mastery of this discipline is a prerequisite for advanced quality maintenance activity as it is practiced in PM Prize-winning facilities.

Previous TPM books published by the Japan Institute of Plant Maintenance have included sections on P-M analysis, but many of our readers have been frustrated by the lack of detailed explanation of its steps. Illustrations of completed analyses have been provided, but not for individual steps. This book thoroughly remedies that deficiency. The first half of *P-M Analysis* clarifies the nature of chronic loss and pinpoints why more traditional approaches have failed. Each step in the process is explained in detail and supported with simple examples and illustrations. The second half of the book offers case studies from several different industries and a practice problem with sample answers critiqued by the authors. The entire book is supported with numerous illustrations and detailed charts for study.

We are very happy to publish this book. It fills a long-acknowledged gap and represents many years of accumulated expertise among its three authors. Kunio Shirose is the original developer of P-M analysis; Yoshifumi Kimura and Mitsugu Kaneda were principal architects of its implementation at prize-winning Nachi-Fujikoshi Corporation, where some of the finest examples of its application have been documented, and where it was incorporated into the Quality Maintenance methodology developed by that company. (Kimura and Kaneda were co-authors of *Training for TPM*, published by Productivity Press, which documents the TPM implementation at Nachi-Fujikoshi.)

Our special thanks to Ed Voigt whose editorial contributions substantially improved and clarified the original text. We also thank translators Andrew Dillon and Bruce Talbot;

---

1. *Systematic failure reduction methods for such environments can be found in other Productivity Press books, including* TPM Development Program, TPM in Process Industries, *and* TPM for Workshop Leaders.

Bill Stanton for cover and page design; Frank Loose Design for composition, layout, and art revisions; Laser Words and Productivity Press India for creating the many figures and tables; Catchword, Inc. for indexing; Vivina Ree for copyediting and proofreading; and Karen Jones for editorial management of the project.

The Problem of Chronic Loss

ELIMINATING QUALITY DEFECTS continues to be a major issue on the shop floor. While few manufacturing operations today have defect rates above 2 or 3 percent, those with rates below 1 percent are probably focused on defects that have become chronic. Unfortunately, chronic problems—whether losses of quality, productivity, or both—just don't seem to go away.

Why do chronic losses persist? This book addresses two reasons why people are unsuccessful in reducing chronic losses:

1. Failure to understand the nature of chronic loss

2. Using ineffective approaches in dealing with chronic losses

CHRONIC LOSSES AND SPORADIC LOSSES

Equipment failures and defects appear in two ways: as sporadic or chronic losses. Sporadic losses indicate sudden, often large deviations from the norm (current performance and quality levels). Chronic losses, on the other hand, indicate smaller, frequent deviations that gradually have been accepted as normal.

Sporadic Losses Are Easy to Correct

Sporadic losses, as the name implies, occur suddenly and infrequently. Typically, they result from a single cause that is relatively easy to identify. Also, because cause-and-effect relationships in sporadic losses are fairly clear, corrective measures are usually easy to formulate.

For example, quality defects may arise when a jig has become abraded to a point where it no longer supports the required precision. Or a spindle may suddenly vibrate excessively, causing unacceptable dimensional variations in the product.

Such problems are usually resolved through measures that restore the process condition or component to its immediately previous state.

Chronic Losses Have Obscure Causes

Chronic losses, on the other hand, live up to their name by resisting a wide variety of corrective measures. They require innovative, "breakthrough" measures that restore the mechanism or component to its *original,* defect-free state.

Unlike sporadic losses, chronic losses are the products of complex, tangled cause-and-effect relationships. Tracking down their causes can be arduous. The reason is simple—chronic losses rarely have just one cause, so it is difficult both to identify causes and to clarify their effects. This makes it equally difficult to devise effective countermeasures (Figure 1-1).

FIGURE 1-1: SPORADIC LOSSES AND CHRONIC LOSSES

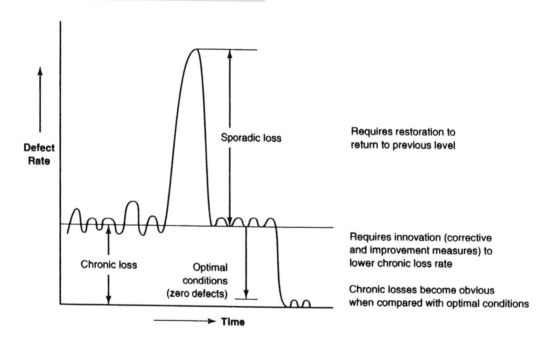

In nearly every case, while countermeasures may bring temporary improvement, the situation gets worse again with time. Eliminating such losses completely is a major challenge—one that conventional approaches can never overcome. What we need are new conceptual tools.

The following sections focus on two issues: how we *think* about chronic losses and how we *address* them.

UNDERSTANDING THE NATURE OF CHRONIC LOSS

Defects and equipment failures persist on the shop floor because people try to tackle chronic losses without understanding what this entails. Grasping the nature of chronic losses is an important prerequisite to eliminating them through improvement.

Broadly speaking, there are two types of chronic loss (Figure 1-2):

Two Types of Chronic Loss

1. *The problem is produced by a single cause, but the cause varies from one occurrence to the next.*

2. *The problem is produced by a combination of causes, which also varies from one occurrence to the next.*

FIGURE 1-2: THE NATURE OF CHRONIC LOSSES

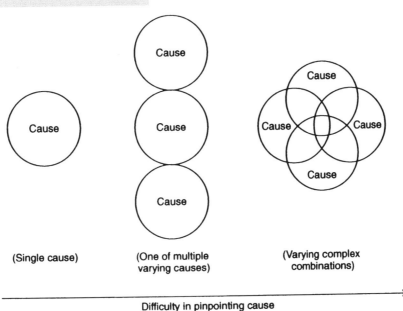

(Single cause)   (One of multiple varying causes)   (Varying complex combinations)

Difficulty in pinpointing cause

Single Causes that Vary Constantly

Suppose for a given problem there are ten potential causes, A through J. Each time the problem occurs, the cause is different. Sometimes it may be A, sometimes C, or D, and so on. Consequently, measures focused on only one specific cause (A, for example) cannot control the problem.

For example, the finishing process which hones inner and outer races in ball bearing housings is critical to the quality of bearings. Consider a situation in which 1 to 2 percent of defects involve roughness in the races. Conditions that could conceivably produce such roughness include a misshapen, poorly mounted, or clogged grindstone; improper dressing; a loose grindstone holder or spindle; and imprecise curve grinding.

Possible causes range from things done in the previous process (such as curve grinding) to actions during the setup procedure (such as attaching the grinder). The actual cause of the defect, however, may change from one instance to the next.

To solve a problem like this the improvement team should examine *all* possible factors and restore them to their original conditions if necessary, while ensuring that correct dimensions and configurations are maintained. These actions are required because while there is no problem when causes can be identified, in practice, identifying them all is often very difficult.

Varying Combinations of Causes

In some cases a combination of multiple and overlapping causes generates the problem. To make matters worse, each time the problem occurs, a different combination of factors may be involved. Today it may be factors A, B, and C; tomorrow A, C, G, and H.

For example, in a polishing process using an internal grinding machine, out-of-roundness defects are sometimes generated by overlapping factors. These can include dimensional variations in the raw material, a worn reference plate on the workpiece mounting surface, vibration in the grindstone spindle, and insufficient quill stiffness. Since all these factors may contribute in combination to any single occurrence of the defect, the team should consider corrective action for all of them, resisting the temptation to target just one.

Failing to appreciate how chronic losses occur is a major obstacle to their elimination. We tend to focus too narrowly on a given cause because we have not sufficiently understood the *phenomenon:* the physical event or precisely what happens to produce the defect in question. Avoiding this common pitfall is essential. Even when the measures taken against a single targeted cause are effective, the improvement is often temporary. The problem will ultimately resurface, because we have failed to eliminate other causes.

PROBLEMS IN REDUCING CHRONIC LOSS

To achieve a lasting reduction in chronic losses we must do three things:

- *Identify* all factors that conceivably contribute to a loss.

- Thoroughly *investigate* each factor.

- *Eliminate* any malfunctions or suboptimal conditions discovered in the process.

Chronic losses persist for another reason. Even when people understand the nature of chronic loss, they continue to use a flawed problem-solving approach. Three types of errors are common in chronic loss analysis:

Common Errors

1. *Phenomena are insufficiently stratified and analyzed.*

2. *Some factors related to individual phenomena are overlooked.*

3. *Abnormalities hidden in individual factors are not addressed.*

Let's look at each situation in more detail.

Phenomena Are Insufficiently Stratified and Analyzed

It is all too easy to find plants where defects and failures are not carefully observed and sufficiently *stratified*, or broken down into discrete and differing aspects. In failing to observe the relevant phenomena carefully, people often do not notice the defect patterns (how), elements (where), and periods (when and how often) that characterize them.

For example, there are several ways that just one phenomenon—dimensional variation—can occur:

- During morning startup

- Before and after blade replacement

- Before and after changeover

- During normal operation

When we focus on the *result*—dimensional variation—without studying the various ways it can appear and the different reasons in each case, it is more difficult to respond intelligently to the reasons behind an individual occurrence. By contrast, once we stratify the phenomenon into types, the causes are easier to identify and appropriate countermeasures are easier to devise.

Many problems remain chronic precisely because people do not thoroughly stratify the phenomena.

Some Factors Related to Individual Phenomena Are Overlooked

Another common weakness in chronic loss analysis is that some potential causes of the phenomena are overlooked and are thus not controlled. Uncontrolled factors can easily lead to chronic losses.

For example, to prevent dimensional variation in external surface grinding with a cylindrical grinder, many causal factors should be controlled. These include chuck precision, center shape abnormalities (wear or damage), horizontal alignment of the chuck and center, and parallelism. Often, however, few or none of these are controlled. For example, slight damage or wear in the center may cause dimensional variation and cylindricality defects but seldom attracts notice. Even if we recognize such factors as sources of quality problems, we may still fail to develop the standards and measurement methods needed to control them.

This is why improvement teams should carefully study all factors related to a chronic loss. Observe the phenomena closely, thoroughly stratify them, and then identify and document all equipment mechanisms involved in their occurrence. Take pains not to overlook any factors that qualify while setting aside those that do not.

Some Abnormalities Hidden in Individual Factors Are Not Addressed

The third weakness in chronic loss problem solving is failing to identify and respond to abnormal conditions within causal factors. Though all causes involve abnormalities, many are left untreated because people literally do not see them. This is especially true of slight abnormalities. Large defects in equipment conditions are obvious to almost everyone. We are more alert to larger problems because they appear more significant. Conversely, the smaller the problem, the more likely we are to ignore it.

THE IMPORTANCE OF SLIGHT ABNORMALITIES

Slight abnormalities in equipment conditions are typically not classified as defects in and of themselves, since their influence on major problems may be quite small. Common examples are dirt, rust, vibration, looseness, wear slightly out of tolerance, or a dirty contact that occasionally malfunctions. But however limited the extent, we must recognize that such conditions do have some influence. For example, even if we do not understand precisely how minor damage and wear in a grinder's center results in dimensional variation, we logically accept that it can happen.

Small Factors Can Have Large Consequences

Employing this logic, consider all potential causes of dimensional variation or of any other quality problem, including the slightest imaginable. Suppose an NC lathe behaves strangely from time to time. Would it be that surprising if a loose screw, rust buildup at a critical location, or a dusty contact turned out to be the single root cause? Slight abnormalities of this kind can have a big impact on equipment operation. For this reason they demand the same treatment as more obvious ones.

Slight abnormalities are often at the root of "function-reduction" (as opposed to "function-loss") breakdowns. The machine itself is not actually down, but its performance falls off because some mechanism or component is malfunctioning. Of course, function-loss breakdowns command far more attention, which is another reason these defects are overlooked.

Cumulative Effects Can Exceed Individual Contributions

In other cases, several slight abnormalities can have a cumulative effect much greater than their individual contributions. Suppose a certain jig has been damaged, but the operator does not notice. He or she keeps using it for assembly work, which results in substandard precision and early wear and eventually causes both static and dynamic imprecision in the equipment.

In another case, a minor variation at one phase of production combines with others scattered throughout the process, resulting in a 1 to 2 percent product defect rate at the end. When ignored, such conditions pose a risk of major equipment defects and breakdowns, as well as quality defects. They also lead to accelerated machine deterioration.

As these examples show, the greater the number of slight abnormalities, the harder it is to pinpoint the sources of whatever problems they collectively cause. Therefore, examine every possible location for defects, from jigs to assembly methods and precision results, to minimize the risk of overlooking even one. A thorough elimination of slight abnormalities is a prerequisite for achieving zero defects and zero breakdowns. Do not underestimate their importance.

OPTIMAL CONDITIONS

A prerequisite to finding and eliminating slight abnormalities is establishing optimal conditions. Slight abnormalities are exposed by comparing the actual state with an ideal or optimal state and highlighting the difference.

Refer to Figure 1-3. Taking the conventional approach, we would judge part A as bad and part B as good. In this case, the standard is based on some previously established level. However, if we look at the problem from a new level—by comparison with optimal conditions—we discover hidden flaws in part B and judge it defective as well. According to this stricter standard, only part C is good.

FIGURE 1-3: STANDARDS BASED ON OPTIMAL LEVELS

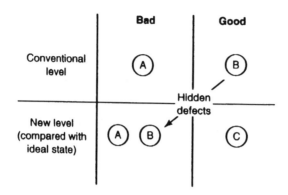

Optimal = Necessary + Desirable

Optimal conditions represent equipment operating at its highest level—reliable, maintainable, performing to the full extent of its design capabilities, and turning out quality results. Optimal conditions are the sum of two categories: necessary and desirable. Necessary conditions are the minimum required to support equipment operation. Desirable conditions are not essential for operation, but they are needed to prevent breakdowns and defects. Optimal conditions therefore include both what a machine must do and what it could do. Consider the examples in Table 1-1.

TABLE 1-1: NECESSARY VS. DESIRABLE CONDITIONS

Mechanism	Necessary	Desirable
Pulley arrangement accommodating three V-belts	• At least one V-belt must be installed for correct operation	• All three V-belts should be installed for operation • All three V-belts should have equal tension • The belts should be free of cracks and grease marks • The pulley should be free of abrasion • The motor and speed reducer should be properly aligned
Grease supply	• Grease must be applied at specific locations	• The grease nipple should be kept clean • The area around the grease fitting should be wiped clean after each application • The condition (color, etc.) and volume level of used lubricant should be checked • Used lubricant should be disposed of properly • The number of days for the lubricant to reach the end of the piping should be estimated • The grease container should be kept clean and free of dirt
Limit switch	• Limit switch must be installed and operated as specified	• The dogs and levers should be aligned in a straight line • Areas around the dogs and levers should allow a lever movement angle of about 30 degrees • The brackets should be tightly fastened

Optimal = Original + Defect-Free

Another way of understanding optimal conditions is "as good as new." Optimal conditions are what the equipment was designed and built for in the first place, and what the manufacturer's manuals reflect. "Optimal" and "original" are in this sense synonymous. Remember that "original" does *not* mean "just before the phenomenon occurred." It means "defect-free"—before chronic losses started to creep in.

USING OPTIMAL CONDITIONS TO EXPOSE SLIGHT ABNORMALITIES

Many manufacturers either (1) do not employ standards based on optimal conditions, or (2) make errors in the way they determine, standardize, or maintain them. Those who operate equipment without knowing its optimal conditions are much more likely to experience breakdowns, defects, and rework. Use optimal conditions to reveal slight abnormalities as follows:

1. Describe the optimal (necessary + desirable) conditions for each function of a given component, making clear the line between normal and abnormal.

2. Compare these to actual conditions. Any variance indicates a slight abnormality.

For example, determine the optimal conditions for a jig in terms of surface roughness, dimensional precision, attachment method, movement, and clamping strength. Then compare these with its present state to see where slight defects have created discrepancies.

FIGURE 1-4: APPROACH TO CHRONIC LOSS REDUCTION

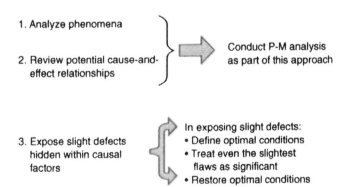

SUMMARY

The following chapters explain how P-M analysis systematically clarifies chronic loss phenomena, identifies causal factors, and guides improvement activities. This is not an "80/20" approach; the aim is *zero* chronic losses. Notice how the word "all" appears in each of these key concepts:

1. **Understand ALL aspects of the phenomenon.** *P-M analysis steps 1 and 2 clarify the phenomenon.*

2. **Review ALL causal factors.** *P-M analysis steps 3 and 4 ensure that the review of factors is thorough and complete.*

3. **Correct ALL abnormalities exposed in the review of factors.** *P-M analysis steps 5 through 8 help teams find, evaluate, correct, and then prevent slight abnormalities in light of optimal conditions*

2 | What Is P-M Analysis?

P-M ANALYSIS IS MORE than an improvement methodology. It is a different way of thinking about problems and the context in which they occur.

To recap from Chapter 1, P-M analysis helps eliminate chronic losses in three stages:

- Look at phenomena analytically and systematically

- Review all causal factors

- Identify all abnormalities and reduce them to zero

The "P" and "M" in P-M analysis do not stand for preventive or productive maintenance. The "P" stands for "phenomenon"—the abnormal event to be controlled. It also stands for "physical"—the perspective we take in viewing the phenomenon. "M" refers to "mechanism," and also to the four production inputs (4Ms) we examine for causal factors: machine (equipment), man (people), material, and method (Figure 2-1). The term "mechanism" applies to any grouping of equipment elements (including jigs and tools) with a common function. It also refers to the "mechanics" or failure mode of an abnormal event.

P-M ANALYSIS DEFINED

P-M analysis *physically analyzes chronic losses according to the inherent principles and natural laws that govern them.* This analysis clarifies the mechanics of their occurrence and the conditions that must be controlled to prevent them.

The basic principle behind P-M analysis is to first understand—in precise physical terms—what happens when a machine breaks down or produces bad parts or material, and how it happens. Only then can we identify and address all causal factors and thus eliminate the chronic loss.

Looking at it another way, P-M analysis is a refined variation of cause-and-effect analysis that considers all causal factors instead of trying to decide which are most influential. Teams using P-M analysis follow this sequence:

1. Physically analyze chronic problems such as defects and failures according to the machine's operating principles.

2. Define the essential or constituent conditions underlying the abnormal phenomena.

3. Identify all factors that logically contribute to the phenomena in terms of the 4Ms: the equipment mechanisms, materials, methods used, and people's actions.

FIGURE 2-1: WHAT IS P-M ANALYSIS?

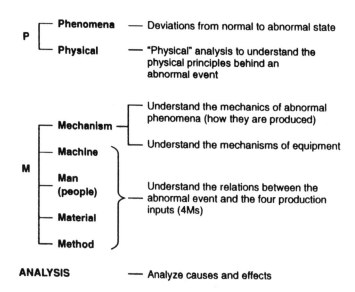

CONVENTIONAL IMPROVEMENT APPROACH

To fully appreciate P-M analysis and what it can do, compare it with the conventional improvement approach.

The QC Model

The conventional improvement approach should be familiar to anyone who has been involved in quality improvement (including QC or quality circle) activities. It generally follows this sequence:

Conventional Improvement Approach

1. *Evaluate current loss picture and select a project theme*

2. *Set improvement targets*

3. *Understand the current situation*

4. *Conduct factor (cause-and-effect) analysis*

5. *Identify and implement countermeasures*

6. *Evaluate results and make required adjustments*

7. *Institute standards and procedures to prevent recurrence*

8. *Reevaluate loss picture and plan for the next project(s)*

This QC model has been widely used on the shop floor, especially where breakdown and defect rates are high. This orthodox, step-by-step method has been very effective in reducing these rates to half or one-third their previous levels.

In most cases, however, almost all the gains come from eliminating sporadic losses, while chronic losses remain. As a result, this conventional approach rarely succeeds in reducing the rate for breakdowns and defects below 1 percent.

Emphasis on Prioritization

Driving this conventional approach is the concept of priority. In other words, teams select improvement projects based on:

- the most numerous or costly defects or failures

- factors having the greatest impact

- the most obvious abnormalities related to those factors

- measures that promise to be most effective (against defects)

Teams use Pareto charts and other tools to identify the most likely factors contributing to breakdowns and defects. Then they implement improvements on a priority basis. They follow up with a survey to find out which improvement measures were most effective (see Figure 2-2).

FIGURE 2-2: THE CONVENTIONAL IMPROVEMENT APPROACH

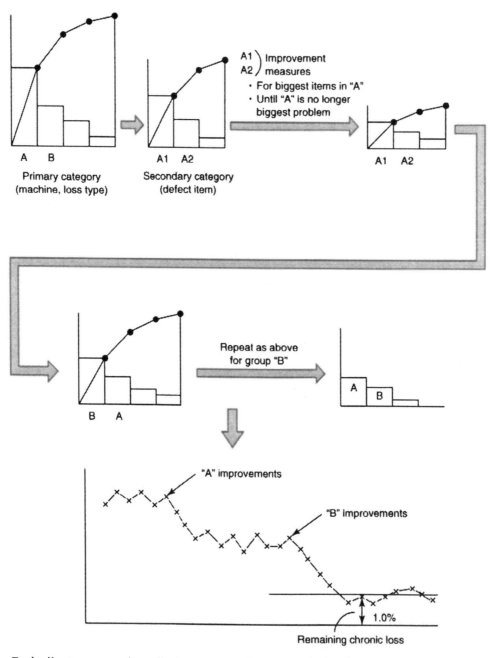

Typically, team members first carry out a Pareto analysis, then extract and stratify the biggest defect items as group "A." Then they study each of the items in this group (A1, A2, etc.) and draft improvement plans.

Next, they follow the same procedure for items in group "B." For both groups, carefully implemented improvement measures will greatly help reduce defects and breakdowns, but they will not completely eliminate them.

The defects or failures that persist can be classified as chronic.

Factor Analysis and Cause-and-Effect Diagrams

Factor analysis, or cause-and-effect analysis, is the process of identifying which factors cause a given problem. Here and throughout this book, it is important to distinguish the terms "factor" and "cause":

> - *FACTOR: any condition that may potentially contribute to the phenomenon.*
>
> - *CAUSE: any factor that immediately precedes the phenomenon and always produces it. For a factor to be a cause it must also be capable of producing the phenomenon by itself.*
>
> - *CAUSAL FACTOR: any factor that contributes to the phenomenon but may or may not directly produce it.*

Figure 2-3 illustrates how factors and causes are related.

Teams use cause-and-effect fishbone diagrams to conduct factor analysis. This analysis helps determine which factors contribute most to producing the defect and should thus be targeted for improvement measures.

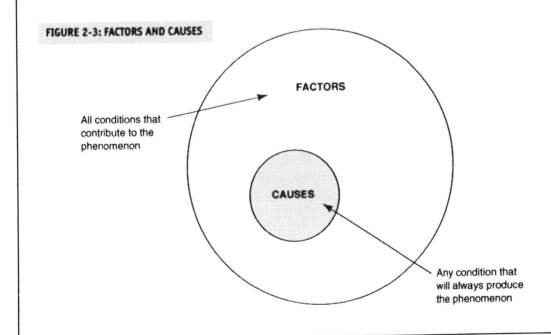

FIGURE 2-3: FACTORS AND CAUSES

FACTORS

All conditions that contribute to the phenomenon

CAUSES

Any condition that will always produce the phenomenon

The cause-and-effect diagram in Figure 2-4 is fairly typical. The team (quality circle, improvement group) uses the 4Ms as categories, and then brainstorms for individual factors within each. Note that some potential causes are listed more than once, which is characteristic for a brainstorming exercise. This approach is both easy to use and effective at the shop floor level. However, it cannot address the chronic losses that block the path to zero defects or zero breakdowns.

Limits of Traditional Factor Analysis

In factor analysis people are encouraged to think up potential causes without first studying equipment mechanisms, structure, or component configurations and functions. Little wonder, then, that under this approach some causal factors are inadvertently omitted. The logical connections between the phenomena and the factors are weak.

Figure 2-4, for example, does not reveal which machining methods were used. We can only guess that the cutting bits used to machine the parts to specified dimensions were fed in automatically rather than manually. Quality awareness, inattention, and other operator factors are cited as potential causes, but if the machining is automated, how can even the most quality-conscious operator affect dimensional accuracy? In that case such factors are irrelevant.

With regard to the equipment, the chart lists factors such as preventive maintenance and checking. It does not indicate, however, which parts of the equipment might have been checked poorly, or which precision checks were so inadequate as to cause dimension defects. Looking strictly at the equipment and jigs/tools areas, we can highlight several flaws in the problem-solving process:

Flaws in Problem Solving Process

- **Crude methods for identifying factors:** *center position (of what?), chucks (which?)*

- **Inclusion of unrelated factors:** *routine and daily checks, parts replacement, materials, deformation (on what basis are these related to the phenomenon?)*

- **Omission of causal factors:** *center shape (friction, damage), vertical and horizontal alignment of chuck and center, loose tailstock (for slide surface), etc.*

- **Logical inconsistency between factors:** *abrasion, wobble (how can something be too tight and too loose at the same time?)*

This is clearly not the best way to pursue causal factors.

FIGURE 2-4: CAUSE-AND-EFFECT DIAGRAM FOR DIMENSIONAL DEFECTS

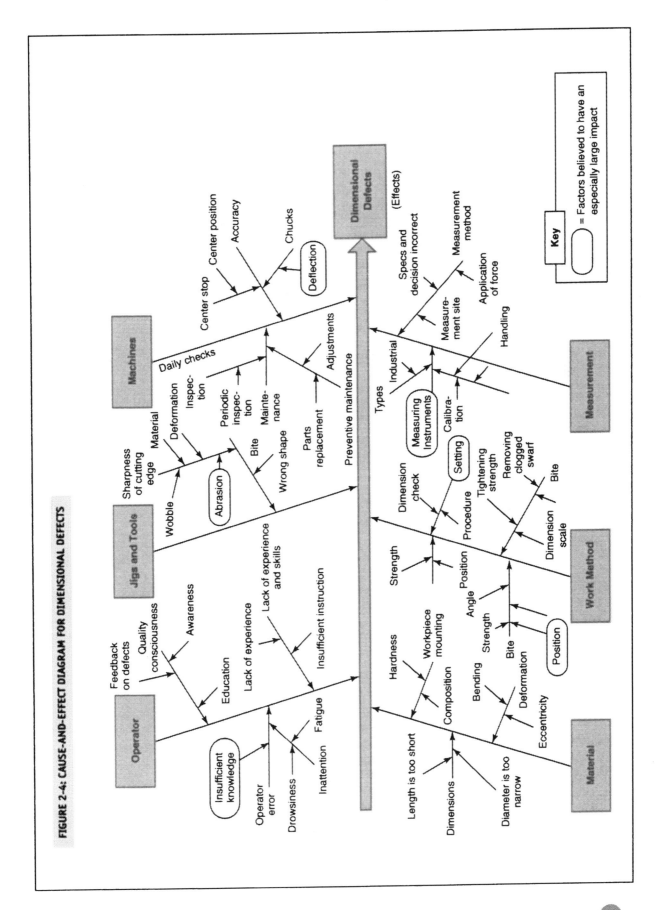

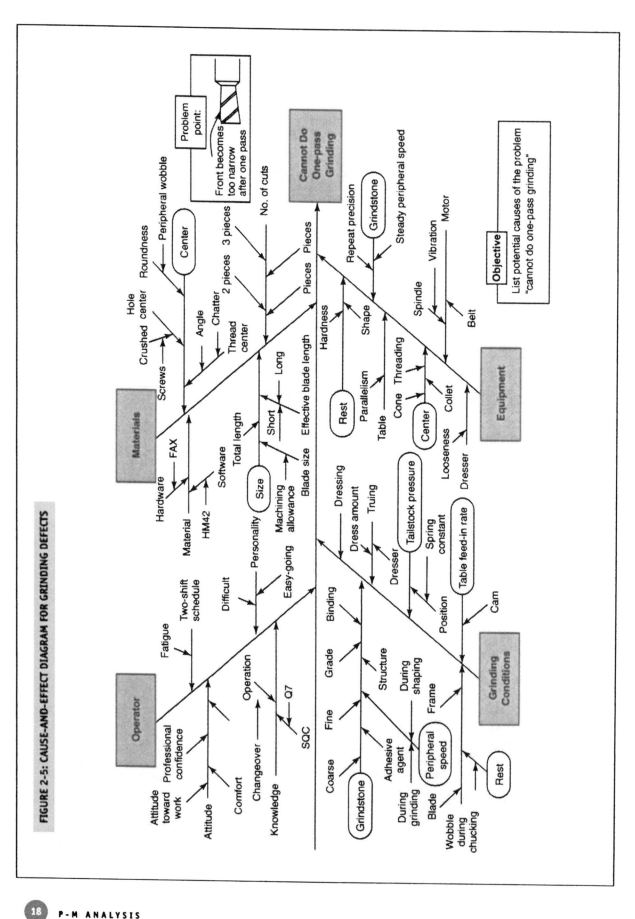

FIGURE 2-5: CAUSE-AND-EFFECT DIAGRAM FOR GRINDING DEFECTS

Figure 2-5 concerns a cylindrical grinder used for peripheral grinding. All loading, machining, and unloading are automatic, and the only human work is changeover.

Here, under the same 4M categories of equipment, materials, methods, and people, suggested obstacles to one-pass grinding include human attitudes (work ethic, comfort, confidence), personality (easygoing, difficult), and fatigue. But are these in fact potential causes? Can having a better attitude toward work or being less fatigued actually make one-pass grinding possible?

Such weak logic commonly appears in cause-and-effect diagrams.

Despite its weaknesses in certain areas, the conventional approach to making improvements is useful and often very effective. Its cardinal weakness is that while it can help *reduce* defects dramatically, it cannot *eliminate* them. Following is a summary of its features:

Conventional Improvement Approach

Objective:
- *Reduce defects to ½ or ⅓ their present level*

Concepts:
- *Priority-based*

- *Focus on factors having the greatest impact*

- *Carry out countermeasures that promise to be most effective*

Methodology:
- *Cause-and-effect diagram*

Application:
- *Use where defect rate is high*

THE NEED FOR A BETTER APPROACH

Like many successful techniques, P-M analysis evolved in response to a need—as a way to eliminate those chronic problems left behind by the conventional improvement approach. In one plant after another that has benefited from the conventional approach, there is still the frustrating inability to drive defects below that 1 percent threshold. As mentioned earlier, the heart of the problem lies in inadequate factor analysis. This weakness exists in every case, regardless of project scope, level of organizational involvement, or enthusiasm of the participants. To reiterate, common flaws in the analysis include crude methods for identifying factors, inclusion of unrelated factors, omission of causal factors, and logical inconsistency between factors.

Why do these kinds of flaws arise? Are there any discernible patterns we can learn to correct? The following reasons stand out most clearly and merit further investigation:

Reasons for Flawed Analysis

- *The machine itself is poorly understood*

- *Phenomena are not considered carefully and logically*

- *Operating principles are not understood*

- *Factors are not understood in sufficient detail*

- *Emphasis on prioritization ignores all but the most influential factors*

The Machine Itself Is Poorly Understood

It is not unusual for the people who should know a machine best to have little knowledge of its inner workings. All too often, improvement groups carry out factor analysis without being able to answer the following questions:

Initial Questions

- *What are the machine's mechanisms and structure?*

- *What kinds of components make up the machine?*

- *What are the functions of those components?*

- *How are the components mounted?*

- *How much precision is required of each component?*

Lack of knowledge of machine mechanisms goes to the heart of why actual causes are overlooked while unrelated factors are included in team analyses. Going back to the example in Figure 2-4, it is probable that little was said about the machining processes because little was *known*. As a result, much time was wasted on irrelevant items.

It is also important to understand which components make up the equipment in question, and how those components are attached or fastened. In some cases this information is decisive for effective factor analysis. For example, answers to the following questions will draw attention to relevant factors and the location of abnormalities:

- "What is this component's function?"
- "Why is this component attached here?"
- "Is this a good mounting method?"
- "Is it OK to have this much friction (or slack)?"

Accordingly, before starting factor analysis, understand the equipment mechanisms, parts configurations, and fastening methods. Sketch them out or study existing drawings to gain an adequate understanding.

Phenomena Are Not Considered Carefully and Logically

In general, the people employing factor analysis do not spend much time looking at phenomena in a careful, logical manner. Instead, they typically describe the phenomenon in simple, general terms and then plunge right into brainstorming, which amounts to "thinking up" factors. Thus, as mentioned previously, unrelated factors may be considered while causal factors are overlooked. The overall scope of factors becomes too narrow, and people tend to draw conclusions based on limited information.

Operating Principles Are Not Understood

Every machine is designed to follow a particular set of operating principles. An operating principle is just as it sounds: the physical explanation of how something works. To use a very mundane illustration, the operating principle behind a pen is that ink from a cartridge flows down with the force of gravity and around a narrow metal tip by capillary action to be absorbed into a finely porous writing surface.

Operating principles are the foundation upon which the machine's mechanisms and structure are developed, and they help clarify physical defect phenomena. And yet, people attempt factor analysis without the slightest understanding of the principles governing their equipment and its mechanisms and components, including control and measurement systems. Important factors are invariably left out when this happens.

Factors Are Not Understood in Sufficient Detail

The next problem arises when factors are selected. Teams frequently lump items under categories that are overbroad. For example, they may consider only major units or mechanisms—tooling, hydraulics, controls, and so forth—instead of individual components. This tends to inhibit detailed analysis. In many cases certain mechanisms are broken down to the component level while others are ignored altogether.

When factors are considered only at the equipment or mechanism level, they end up being too general. Teams may need to break down categories even further into component characteristics such as strength, shape and texture, dimensional accuracy, and means of attachment.

Emphasis on Prioritization Ignores All but the Most Influential Factors

Prioritization is a very natural and necessary process. Many project teams start by identifying what they consider the most influential factors and focus their countermeasures accordingly. As a result, however, other factors are not addressed. While prioritization can be very effective in reducing high defect rates, it cannot eliminate them completely.

Moreover, unless team members can see a clear physical difference between more or less influential factors, they often base distinctions on intuition, or on whatever factors come to mind first. This subjective "filtering" is particularly inappropriate in dealing with chronic quality defects, where the identity and relative impact of causal factors are often obscure. These are some of the unintended consequences:

Results of Subjective Analysis

- *A causal factor is ruled out because it rarely occurs*

- *A causal factor is ruled out because its impact appears small*

- *A causal factor is ruled out because it was not influential before*

- *A factor is deemed influential because it was relevant in a previous case*

HOW P-M ANALYSIS WORKS TO ELIMINATE CHRONIC LOSSES

In addressing chronic losses under P-M analysis, do *not* attempt to isolate the most influential factors—do not prioritize.

Why? Because it is very rare that a recurring defect or malfunction is clearly attributable to one, two, or even several distinct causes. Instead, we typically encounter a tangled web of factors that may or may not be contributors. Rather than prioritizing, consider—logically and with equal emphasis—*all* factors that might have an impact on the chronic defect. Then within each factor seek out every abnormality, no matter how small, and arrive at appropriate countermeasures for each.

The following five concepts are essential for achieving zero defects:

Keys to Zero Defects

- *Consider all causal factors*

- *Investigate all causal factors thoroughly for abnormalities*

- *Correct all abnormalities*

- *Correct abnormalities* together

- *Repeat the process if results are unsatisfactory*

Consider All Causal Factors

The persistence of defects, breakdowns and other losses is proof that those responsible have overlooked at least some contributing factors or deficiencies lurking within factors. Hence the need to thoroughly review all causal factors. This means studying each of the machine's mechanisms, its structure, and its components—as well as materials, methods, and people—to make sure nothing has been missed.

Investigate All Causal Factors Thoroughly for Abnormalities

Thoroughly investigate all factors you list. While such an effort may seem time consuming and costly, the alternative—a piecemeal approach—simply will not do the job. Identifying and correcting two or three major items solves only part of the problem. In fact, any reduction in the loss rate will later level off or even reverse itself because other hidden factors were not addressed. Before long you are back where you started. Instead, investigate each causal factor to see if anything is actually wrong.

Correct *All* Abnormalities

Common abnormalities may include the following, whether for integral components or for add-on components:

Common Abnormalities

- *Deviation from current standard values*

- *Deviation from provisional values where there are no permanent standards*

- *Deviation from a component's normal observed function or its desired function where there are no provisional or permanent standards*

- *Slight abnormalities that may or may not involve deviation from a component's normal or desired function*

Sometimes a poor selection of standards and/or measurement methods can hinder the process of sorting out these abnormalities. Make sure the measurement methods you select are adequate for the task.

Having identified as many abnormalities as possible, correct them all without regard to which may contribute most to defects. To reduce losses to zero, even apparently minor problems must be corrected.

Correct Abnormalities Together

Most people make one change at a time and then examine the results. Once all corrections have been made, they standardize those that were successful. Ten abnormalities would thus translate into ten iterations of the correcting/checking process. While there is nothing inherently wrong with this approach, it does not work very well for chronic losses where the cause-and-effect relationships are complex or constantly changing. For example, addressing one item may alter the influence of another.

Instead, correct all abnormalities simultaneously. This saves time and reduces the chance of a factor being overlooked. This strategy is one of the most distinctive features of P-M analysis in contrast with the conventional improvement approach.

Arguably, correcting deficiencies together prevents us from isolating the effects of individual actions. However, since chronic defects rarely have clearly definable causes, there is little point in trying to determine which countermeasure had which effect. We rarely know at any given time whether a machine is malfunctioning due to just one of many potential causes or to the combined effect of multiple causes. It is difficult to accurately gauge the influence of any particular factor. The effects of correcting abnormalities together can be standardized as long as nondefective conditions can be maintained (i.e., without variation in the causal factors).

Repeat the Process if Results Are Unsatisfactory

What if, after all improvements have been made, the results are not satisfactory? No approach, including P-M analysis, guarantees immediate perfection. Chronic defects linger for a variety of reasons:

P-M Analysis Is Unsuccessful When. . .

- *Some factors were overlooked*

- *Abnormalities were not thoroughly identified (scope of search was too broad or overlooked some items)*

- *Accepted standard values are incorrect or inappropriate*

- *Measurement methods are incorrect or inappropriate*

- *The countermeasures themselves contained errors*

Starting over again can be frustrating, but there is no choice if you are committed to zero defects. Of course, in most cases the second analysis should take less time and effort, because fewer abnormalities are left to correct.

In summary, the key features of a zero defects improvement strategy are as follows:

Zero Defects Strategy

Objectives:
- *Long term: to reach "zero"*
- *Short term: to get as close as possible to "zero"*

Concepts:
- *Do not use priority-based approach*
- *Think logically and list all causal factors behind the defects*
- *Investigate all factors*
- *Correct all abnormalities*
- *Try to correct abnormalities together*
- *Institute or revise standards as needed to prevent abnormalities from recurring*
- *Be thorough in all the above*

Methodology:
- *P-M analysis*

Application:
- *Use where defect rate is low*
- *Use where remaining defects are chronic*

USING THE CONVENTIONAL IMPROVEMENT APPROACH AND P-M ANALYSIS TOGETHER

The conventional improvement approach and P-M analysis can be used together to produce good results as follows: In areas where the defect or failure rate is high, first implement the conventional (priority-based) improvement approach to greatly reduce the loss rate. Thereafter, follow up by implementing the zero defect strategy described above. (See Figure 2-6.) Adopting this zero-defect strategy too early—when the defect rate is high—is likely to be time-consuming and unproductive. However, if after diligent application the conventional approach proves ineffective, it may be necessary to start over with P-M analysis.

FIGURE 2-6: WHEN TO APPLY P-M ANALYSIS

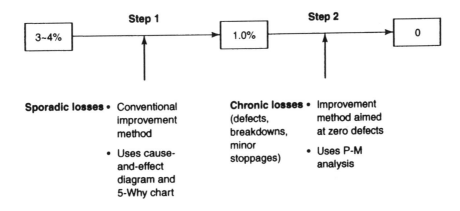

Sporadic losses • Conventional improvement method

• Uses cause-and-effect diagram and 5-Why chart

Chronic losses (defects, breakdowns, minor stoppages) • Improvement method aimed at zero defects

• Uses P-M analysis

Handling Multiple Projects

Figure 2-7 illustrates how P-M analysis can be used on successive projects to move from a 1 percent defect rate to zero defects. Start by arranging all chronic loss items on a Pareto chart and singling out the biggest item (A). Using P-M analysis, survey all causal factors and make improvements to eliminate defects. Next, repeat this process for item B, then item C, and so on until chronic losses are eradicated.

FIGURE 2-7: ACHIEVING ZERO DEFECTS BY ELIMINATING CHRONIC LOSS

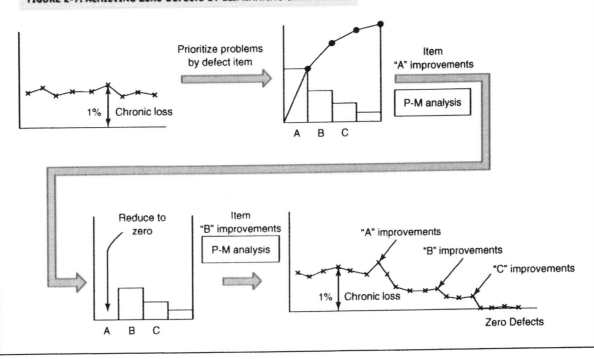

Note the point where both approaches are in agreement. In selecting the project, priority is placed on the machine and/or loss categories with greatest impact on plant performance. It is only in the analysis—after a project has been selected—that P-M analysis avoids prioritization.

Table 2-1 provides a feature-by-feature comparison of P-M analysis and the conventional improvement approach.

TABLE 2-1: P-M ANALYSIS VS. CONVENTIONAL APPROACH

Approach	Conventional Approach	P-M Analysis
Objective	Reduce defects to $\frac{1}{2}$ or $\frac{1}{3}$ their present level	Reduce defects to zero or get as close as possible
Concepts	• Priority-based • Focus on factors having the greatest impact • Carry out measures only on selected factors	• Not priority-based • Think logically; list all possible factors behind defects • Investigate all factors • Correct all abnormalities
Methodology	Cause-and-effect diagrams	P-M Analysis
Application	• Use where defect rate is high • Helps eliminate sporadic losses	• Use where defect rate is low • Helps eliminate chronic losses

THE ZERO DEFECTS PHILOSOPHY

More than mere technique is necessary for P-M analysis to succeed. Technique must be accompanied by a philosophy and attitude that accept nothing less than perfection as the ultimate goal. Coupled with this attitude is the realization that perfection is a long-term process. Applying P-M analysis to eliminate all chronic losses on one critical machine requires patience and persistence. Most likely there will be obstacles along the way, along with a dead end or two.

Confidence to succeed builds gradually through the repeated practice of a proven approach. But none of this will happen unless teams have a crystal clear sense of purpose: that they can and must attain zero defects. So stick with this improvement philosophy until you have mastered it. It will be your most important resource.

3 Fundamentals of Physical Analysis

THE LAST CHAPTER EXAMINED the theory and rationale behind P-M analysis as an approach to eliminating chronic losses. The actual steps are as follows:

P-M Analysis Steps

1. *Clarify the phenomenon*

2. *Conduct a physical analysis*

3. *Identify constituent conditions*

4. *Study 4Ms for causal factors*

5. *Set optimal conditions and standards*

6. *Plan and conduct a survey of factors*

7. *Identify abnormalities to be addressed*

8. *Propose and make improvements*

While each step is important, Step 2, "Conduct a physical analysis," is critical to the success of P-M analysis. When you understand this step, the others fall into place more easily. This chapter explains how physical analysis bridges the gap between known phenomena and causal factors. Chapter 4 reviews the entire P-M analysis process.

WHAT IS PHYSICAL ANALYSIS?

Physical analysis is a logical investigation of phenomena such as defects or breakdowns that explains how the phenomena occur in terms of physical principles and quantities. "Physics" refers to the physical processes and phenomena of a given machine or system. "To analyze" means to break down a whole into its component parts and to learn their nature and relationships. Hence, *physical analysis* uses a machine's operating principles to clarify how various parts of a machine interact to generate abnormal phenomena.

Abnormal phenomena that occur on the shop floor are those that deviate from what is normal or expected. Therefore, the first step in physical analysis is to analyze this deviation. We do not look for the cause of the deviation. Rather, we study the physical and/or chemical changes that constitute the deviation.

For a more concrete understanding of what is meant by "physical analysis," consider the following examples:

- *Example 1: Damaged workpiece(s)*
  The damage is a deformation that tends to occur in a relatively soft object (material with less surface strength) due to impact with a harder object.

- *Example 2: Blown fuse*
  The phenomenon of a blown fuse occurs when a current exceeds the rated level for longer than the specified time and in the process melts the fuse.

- *Example 3: Variation in finish dimensions*
  On a lathe, variation in finish dimensions occurs when there is variation in the distance between the blade of the cutting tool and the reference position of the workpiece.

FIGURE 3-1: ABNORMAL PHENOMENON = DEVIATION

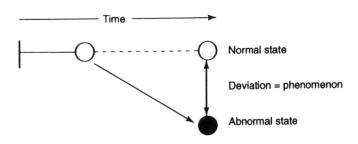

Physical Analysis Explains How, Not Why

As these examples illustrate, physical analysis means logically explaining *how* a phenomenon occurred; it does not necessarily explain *why*. Physical analysis is a bridge that helps us draw logical relationships between phenomena and their potential causes.

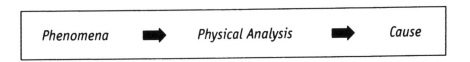

Here are two good reasons for carrying out physical analyses:

1. The outcome of physical analysis determines how we look for causal factors. If our physical analysis is in error, we may overlook some of these factors.

2. Correct physical analysis also helps us avoid pursuing factors that are irrelevant.

EXAMPLES OF PHYSICAL ANALYSIS

The following examples illustrate common mistakes in physical analysis.

Problem 1: Match Doesn't Light

FIGURE 3-2: MATCH DOES NOT LIGHT

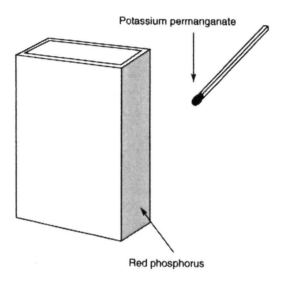

Potassium permanganate

Red phosphorus

Refer to Figure 3-2. Students making a physical analysis of this phenomenon observed the following:

- Matchstick is moist

- Tip of matchstick (potassium permanganate) is too small

- Match tip is worn down

- Match is struck with insufficient force

- Match is struck at incorrect angle

These are all potential causes—reasons why the match won't light. None of them explains the physical principles behind this deviation from the norm. As explained in Chapter 2, brainstorming for causes is not desirable when dealing with chronic loss. It tends to cut short the investigation into causal factors.

Before conducting a physical analysis, we must understand the match's ignition principles. A match lights when sufficient friction heat builds up between the red phosphorus on the match-box and the potassium permanganate on the matchstick. A correct physical analysis of this problem would describe the phenomenon as follows:

> **Physical Analysis**
>
> *The match does not ignite because friction heat is insufficient.*

Problem 2: Bicycle Brakes Poorly

FIGURE 3-3: BYCYCLE BRAKES FUNCTION POORLY

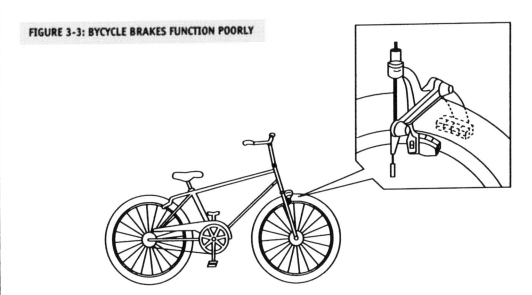

Physical analysis of a bicycle's poor braking yielded the following observations:

• Rubber brake pads are worn

• Rubber brake pads do not meet the wheel at the proper angle

• Rubber brake pads are contaminated with oil and dirt

• Brake cable is extended

As in the previous example, this is not a physical analysis. These are only potential causes of poor braking. A proper physical analysis of this phenomenon would be more like this:

Physical Analysis

Due to insufficient friction resistance, the brakes do not provide enough torque to control the bicycle's speed.

Problem 3: Variation in Width Dimension

FIGURE 3-4: VARIATION IN WIDTH DIMENSION

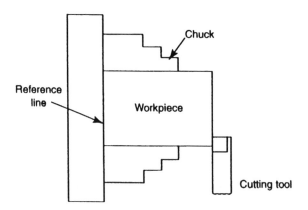

A physical analysis of excessive variation in the width of parts turned on a lathe revealed the following:

- Variation between the part reference line and the finished surface

- Looseness in the table slide mechanism

- Change in contact points between cutting tool and workpiece

- Part does not fit with stop

- Weak chuck

- Stop not set at proper angle

- Part not handled correctly

- Change in cutting tool position relative to the part reference line

The first item, "Variation between the part reference line and the finished surface," only rephrases the phenomenon. All the rest are potential causes except for the last item, *"change in cutting tool position relative to the part reference line."* This is a true physical analysis, explaining precisely what happened to produce the phenomenon.

AVOID ERRORS IN PHYSICAL ANALYSIS

As mentioned earlier, a mistake in the physical analysis can lead to mistakes in defining the causal factors. These factors will normally be investigated at three levels: constituent conditions, primary 4M correlations, and secondary 4M correlations. (The number of levels may vary with equipment complexity.) Constituent conditions are those that alone or in combination with others can bring about the phenomenon. 4M correlations are the factors behind these constituent conditions found in equipment, materials, methods, and people. (Chapter 4 will address all these factors in detail under Steps 3 and 4 of the P-M analysis process.)

In Table 3-1, the shaded example illustrates how mistaking a potential cause for a physical analysis of the problem limits the factors explored. The difference in this case is between two potential causes and seven—which could mean the difference between solving the problem partially or completely.

TABLE 3-1: CORRECT AND INCORRECT PHYSICAL ANALYSIS

Abnormal phenomenon: Poor flow of parts from feeder		
Physical Analysis	**Constituent Conditions**	**Primary 4M Correlation**
Insufficient vibration in feeder	1. Defective calibration of variable resistor	1.1 Incorrect calibration
	2. Defect due to gap in flat spring	2.1 Large gap in flat spring
Friction force of part against contact surface is greater than force of moving part	1. Insufficient feeder vibration	1.1 Defective calibration of variable resistor 1.2 Large gap in flat spring
	2. Shape of workpiece cut edge is incorrect	2.1 Cut edge has too much burr 2.2 Cut edge is damaged from being dropped
	3. Defective shape of feeder transfer surface	3.1 Damage or wear on feeder transfer surface
	4. Too many parts in feeder	4.1 Defective adjustment of capacity limiter
	5. Parts feeder is not level	5.1 Loose leveling bolt

In summary, these are some of the mistakes teams commonly make when carrying out physical analysis:

Common Mistakes

- *Describing (rephrasing) the phenomena*

- *Mistaking a constituent condition for a physical analysis*

- *Providing more than one physical analysis*

- *Listing only some of the causal factors*

Physical Analysis Requires a Clearly Defined Phenomenon

There is only one physical analysis for any phenomenon. When teams come up with several analyses, they probably have not defined the phenomenon narrowly enough. This can create problems. Physical analysis of a phenomenon too broadly defined will yield too many causal factors. As a result, teams will be unable to distinguish the key points.

Unfortunately, some teams and team members shrink from physical analysis because it seems technically intimidating. However, as the preceding examples show, physical analysis is not complicated. Once teams work through one or two analyses of problems in their areas, they get used to the process. Make a habit of thinking logically and physical analysis will eventually come naturally and easily.

CONDUCTING A PHYSICAL ANALYSIS

Physical analysis consists of four steps:

Four Steps of Physical Analysis

1. *Identify basic operating principles*

2. *Identify operating standards*

3. *Identify interacting elements*

4. *Quantify physical changes*

Identify Operating Principles

Whether equipment is manual, semiautomatic, or automatic, it runs according to a set of basic operating principles. In the case of general purpose machine tools, most operators understand how the main unit operates but know surprisingly little about peripheral mechanisms such as hydraulic systems. In the case of NC machines, many operators do not understand the control or measurement principles. If team members do not understand the operating principles for a machine or component, however, they cannot conduct a physical analysis. One or more of these principles apply uniquely to the actual phenomenon. So first review all operations and understand the principles that apply.

Identify Operating Standards

Next, identify those operating standards associated with the normal (defect-free) state. There are actually two parts to this step:

1. Relate the operating principles to equipment mechanisms

2. Identify how those mechanisms should normally function for the phenomenon *not* to occur

Processing principles manifest in the equipment mechanisms, so identify which principles are reflected in the relevant mechanisms and which parts of the mechanisms are most important in understanding how the phenomenon occurred. Then consider what standards should apply to prevent defects or failures from occurring. For example, the operating principles behind the arc welding process include:

- creating an arc in an inert gas between the base material and the electrode

- using the heat of the arc to melt and fuse (weld) the base material

The operating standards (to prevent defects) are as follows:

- Do not allow the current to fluctuate during welding

- Maintain a constant distance between the electrode and the base material

- Maintain the electrode at the specified angle when moving it forward to weld along the base material

Identify Interacting Elements

Deviations can result from a combination of malfunctions, so identify what interacting elements—equipment, tooling, and workpiece—are involved and what changes occur. For example, consider the relation between the position of the workpiece and the position of the tool, and how each changes to produce an abnormal result. Making a sketch of how these elements move in relation to each other may clarify the mechanics behind the phenomenon.

Quantify Physical Changes

Next, consider what physical, measurable changes take place when the phenomenon occurs. Think about appropriate measurement units to quantify the change in each pair of correlating elements that accompanies the phenomenon. Stick with fundamental units such as distance, mass, time, speed, temperature, resistance, and so on. These units fall under four types: basic, absolute, thermal, and electrical (Table 3-2). In the match-lighting example discussed earlier, the physical principles can be explained in terms of a thermal unit (thermal volume Q). In other words, the problem is one of insufficient thermal volume Q (Kcal) for match ignition.

THE LOGICAL FLOW OF PHYSICAL ANALYSIS

Figure 3-5 illustrates, in flowchart form, how all the elements in physical analysis fit together logically. There are actually two flows involved. Running from top to bottom is the physical development of the phenomenon in question, from equipment design theory to process results. The actual flow of physical analysis runs from left to right.

Most of the items in Figure 3-5 are change *inputs*. Machine design is based on certain operating principles, along with principles of *measurement* and *control*. Along with those principles there must be *operating standards* that will define original, defect-free conditions. These principles and standards are used to develop all the functioning *mechanisms*, which in turn determine the machine's *structure* and its various *components*. These physical elements are necessary for *machine operation*. The *output* is either *normal*, *defect-free* results or an *abnormal phenomenon* (quality defects or equipment failure).

Physical analysis examines each of these machine and process inputs, with other physical elements—*tooling, part/material, process parameters*—and the phenomenon itself to understand the *change (deviation)* that has occurred. What remains is *identifying the interacting elements* and *quantifying the physical changes* associated with the phenomenon.

TABLE 3-2: SYMBOLS AND UNITS FOR PHYSICAL QUANTITIES

Unit	Physical Quantity	Symbol	Unit (MKS)	
Basic	Length	L, l	m	$1 \text{ m} = 10^2 \text{ cm} = 10^3 \text{ mm} = 10^6 \mu = 10^{10} \text{Å}$
	Mass	M, m	kg	$1 \text{ kg} = 10^3 \text{ g} = 10^6 \text{ mg}$
	Time	T, t	s	$3600 \text{ s} = 1\text{h}$
Absolute	Area	A, S	m^2	$1 \text{ m}^2 = 10^4 \text{ cm}^2$
	Volume	V, v	m^3	$1 \text{ m}^3 = 10^6 \text{ cm}^3$
	Density	ρ	kg/m^3	$1 \text{ kg/m}^3 = 10^{-3} \text{ g/cm}^3$
	Speed	v, u, V	m/s	$1 \text{ m/s} = 10^2 \text{ cm/s}$
	Acceleration	a, α	m/s^2	$1 \text{ m/s}^2 = 10^2 \text{ cm/s}$
	Force	F, f	$\text{N (m·kg/s}^2)$	$1 \text{ N} = 10^5 \text{ dyn}$, 1kg mass = 9.8 N
	Moment of force	M	N·m	
	Radian	θ, ϕ	r a d	$1 \text{ rad} = 57° \; 18'$, $2\pi \text{ rad} = 360°$
	Steradian	ω	r a d/s	
	Angular acceleration	ω, α	r a d/s^2	
	Moment of inertia	I	kg·m^2	
	Angular momentum	$I \omega$	$\text{kg·m}^2/\text{s}^2$	
	Frequency	n, f, ν	Hz (1/s)	
	Momentum	mv	m·kg/s	$1\text{m kg/s} = 1 \text{ N·s} = 10^5 \text{ cm·g/s}$
				$1\text{J} = 10^7 \text{ erg}$, 1kg mass · m = 9.8J
	Work (energy, heat)	W	$\text{J (m}^2\text{kg/s}^2)$	$1\text{eV} = 1.60 \times 10^{-19} \text{ J}$
	Power	P	$\text{W (m}^2\text{kg/s}^3)$	$1\text{W} = 10^7 \text{ erg/s}$, 1PS = 735 W
Thermal	Temperature	t	° C	
	Thermodynamic temperature	T	° K	0° K = −273° C
	Quantity of heat	Q	kcal	$1\text{kcal} = 10^3 \text{ cal}$
	Specific heat	c	kcal/kg·deg	1kcal/kg·deg = 1cal/g·deg
Electrical	Quantity of electricity (electric charge)	Q, q	C	
	Electric field strength	E	V/m	1 V/m = 1 N/C
	Electric potential	V	V	
	Electromotive force	E	V	
	Capacitance	C	F	
	Current	I, i	A	
	Electric resistance	R, r	Ω	
	Resistivity	ρ	$\Omega \cdot \text{m}$	
	Electric power	P	W	
	Magnetic field strength	H	A/m	
	Magnetic flux density	B	Wb/m^2 (N/A·m)	
	Magnetic flux	$\downarrow$	Wb	
	Impedance	L, M	H	

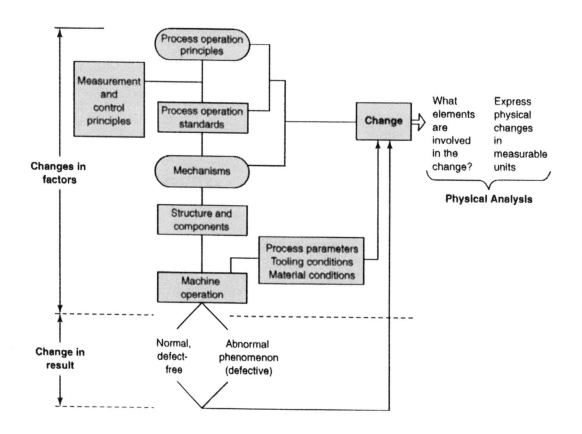

FIGURE 3-5: DEVELOPMENT AND ANALYSIS OF ABNORMAL PHENOMENON

SUMMARY

Table 3-3 lists the results of two physical analyses, showing the relationship among operating principles, interacting elements, and quantifiable physical changes. When teams master this analytical technique, they can consistently pinpoint what happens to produce abnormal (off-standard) phenomena. From that point they can logically identify causal factors and specific abnormalities, then generate appropriate countermeasures.

TABLE 3-3: EXAMPLES OF PHYSICAL ANALYSIS

| | Operating Principles | Operating Standards | Physical Analysis | |
			Interacting Elements	Quantifiable Changes
1. Flashlight does not work	• Current flow in resistor wire causes thermal effect and lamp lights when temperature reaches 1000°C	• Battery's electrostatic value must be no higher than the rated value • There must be sufficient contact between battery and filament • Bulb should not be burned out	• Between battery and filament	• Current not sufficient to light bulb
2. Blown fuse	• An electric charge with a higher-than-rated current value passes through fuse (a weak connection point) for more than the allowable time, causing heat to build up until fuse blows and breaks circuit	• Total electric charge must remain constant • Electric current must remain constant • The fuse capacitance must be from 3-5× rated current value	• Between equip-ment and fuse	• Excess current (above rated value) caused heat (joules) to rise until it melted fuse

4 Implementing P-M Analysis Step-by-Step

THE LAST CHAPTER EXPLAINED that the basic approach in P-M analysis is to stratify abnormal phenomena correctly, understand the relevant operating principles and mechanisms, and analyze them from a physical perspective. The next step is to list and investigate all logically plausible factors, regardless of the degree to which they appear to contribute to the problem, and eliminate all abnormalities through effective countermeasures and controls (Figure 4-1).

This chapter reviews the entire P-M analysis process in detail. As you work through the steps, pay particular attention to the following aspects which have proven most crucial to its success:

- Defining the phenomenon

- Understanding the mechanisms and structure of the equipment

- Physically analyzing the phenomenon

- Managing to sustain improvements

OVERVIEW

Step 1 involves a rigorous study of the equipment's operating principles, mechanisms, and structure. This forms the basis for understanding and analyzing the phenomenon from a physical perspective in Step 2. As we have already established, Step 2 is critical. How teams view the equipment physically will strongly influence the way they address causes.

In Step 3 we identify all conditions that may logically bring about or "constitute" the phenomenon. Then we look at how these constituent conditions correlate with the 4Ms (equipment, materials, methods, and people) and list all conceivable factors in Step 4. Through Steps 5, 6, and 7, respectively, we determine optimal standards, conduct an on-site survey to evaluate each factor, and document even the slightest defects we find. Finally, in Step 8 we make improvements for each abnormality and institute strict controls to sustain optimal conditions.

This chapter reviews each of these steps in detail.

FIGURE 4-1: STEPS IN P-M ANALYSIS

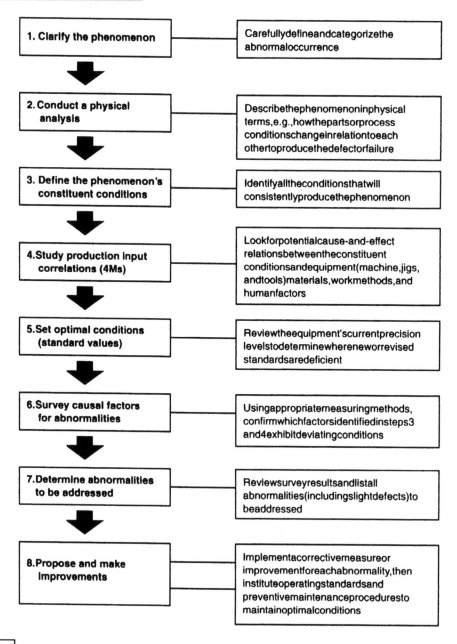

| 1. Clarify the phenomenon | Carefully define and categorize the abnormal occurrence |

| 2. Conduct a physical analysis | Describe the phenomenon in physical terms, e.g., how the parts or process conditions change in relation to each other to produce the defect or failure |

| 3. Define the phenomenon's constituent conditions | Identify all the conditions that will consistently produce the phenomenon |

| 4. Study production input correlations (4Ms) | Look for potential cause-and-effect relations between the constituent conditions and equipment (machine, jigs, and tools) materials, work methods, and human factors |

| 5. Set optimal conditions (standard values) | Review the equipment's current precision levels to determine where new or revised standards are deficient |

| 6. Survey causal factors for abnormalities | Using appropriate measuring methods, confirm which factors identified in steps 3 and 4 exhibit deviating conditions |

| 7. Determine abnormalities to be addressed | Review survey results and list all abnormalities (including slight defects) to be addressed |

| 8. Propose and make improvements | Implement a corrective measure or improvement for each abnormality, then institute operating standards and preventive maintenance procedures to maintain optimal conditions |

Step 1: CLARIFY THE PHENOMENON

The Japanese equivalent of "phenomenon" means "an occurrence or fact that can be observed; the outward manifestation of a thing, as opposed to its essence." In turn, "observation" is defined as "seeing through to the essential nature of a thing; grasping the entirety of its physical appearance." So if we are to grasp the essence of a problem, we must observe it closely and understand what we see. Indeed, half the problem is solved once we grasp it accurately.

In P-M analysis, "clarifying the phenomenon" means using our observation skills to grasp facts and illuminate underlying concepts. Without this vital step, P-M analysis may end up missing the mark.

Observe *How* the Phenomenon Occurs *Where* It Occurs

To avoid acting on unfounded assumptions, observe the phenomenon live on the shop floor. Assumptions and suppositions do not define phenomena; they only block solutions. "Verify it with your own eyes" should be a slogan for problem solving.

Merely looking at the scene of a problem is not enough, however. These are some of the questions teams should ask when observing phenomena:

1. During what specific machine operation (drilling, boring, grinding) does the phenomenon occur?

2. Does it always occur under the same circumstances (morning startup, before or after changeover, long runs)?

3. Does it occur at regular or irregular intervals?

4. Does it get better or worse over time?

5. Does it occur on more than one machine?

6. Does it occur only for certain operators?

Adopting this perspective places the phenomenon in sharp focus and helps teams understand it properly.

How Clear Must We Make the Phenomenon?

If the goal is to eliminate chronic losses completely, we need to stratify phenomena into the smallest verifiable units. Why? So that we leave no stone unturned in looking for causal factors.

In other words, be specific. Phrases such as "scratches occur," "a lot of operating defects show up," or "nuisance stoppages happen" are too vague. When an automatic bolt-tightening device stops frequently, for example, we need to state this precisely: "the machine sometimes shuts down when bolts are not fed in", or "the machine occasionally shuts down when bolts are fed in at an angle and fail to enter the holes."

Keep asking why

To this end, it is helpful to ask *why* at least three times when defining a phenomenon or selecting an improvement theme. Asking *why* helps us define the phenomenon precisely enough that people attempting the improvement can conceive the possibility of zero losses.

Consider the statement "minor stoppages happen." A team would be hard-pressed to find the best point to concentrate its efforts in achieving "zero minor stoppages." Instead, start by asking, "Why are there minor stoppages?" Assume one answer is, "because parts keep jamming the chute," then ask, "*Why* do parts keep jamming the chute?"

"Because the feed rate is too high."

"Why is the feed rate too high?"

"Because the drive motor sometimes speeds up," and so forth.

In this manner, team members clarify the scope of the problem considerably and make their task a lot more manageable.

Aim for zero

Just as we pursue "zero" objectives in setting TPM improvement targets, we need to set "zero occurrence" targets for improvements relating to chronic defects. Remember that optimal conditions include what is desirable, not just what is necessary.

In the example just given, the target would be "zero speed variation in the conveyor belt drive motor." The quickest way to cut chronic losses is by executing successive projects that assume that zero losses can be achieved. A series of smaller projects is far more effective than a major, broadbrush improvement strategy with unrealistic targets.

Even if your overall objective is to cut losses by half, try to achieve that goal through a series of individual projects that each have credible, verifiable zero-loss objectives. Pursue perfection one chronic loss at a time.

How to Grasp Phenomena

Stratify phenomena down to the smallest verifiable unit using such tools as magnifying glasses, microscopes, and roundness gauges. For example, are scratches caused by striking or abrasion? Does an out-of-roundness defect mean just barely? A squashed circle? Or a polyhedron? Be more specific than the designation "out of round" and identify exactly the shape observed.

```
┌─────────────────────────────────────────────────────────┐
│  Specifying Defect Phenomena                            │
│                                                          │
│    • Scratches: blows, scrapes, gouges                  │
│                                                          │
│    • Out-of-roundness: ovoid, triangular, polyhedral    │
│                                                          │
│    • Tip wear: chipping, relief surface wear, rake surface wear │
│                                                          │
└─────────────────────────────────────────────────────────┘
```

Another crucial point, as we have already seen, is verifying the phenomenon with one's own eyes. Hearsay should never be taken at face value and suppositions should never guide judgments. One look is worth a thousand rumors.

Procedures for Defining Phenomena

Defining phenomena means correctly understanding and sorting them by type or pattern based on what they consist of, how they occur, where they occur, what kind of machines are involved, and so on. As shown in Table 4-1, the crucial points in this process are:

- Eliminating preconceived notions

- Carefully observing and analyzing the facts *onsite*

- Sorting and stratifying phenomena thoroughly (5Ws and 1H)

- Comparing the normal (good products) with the abnormal (defective products) to pinpoint all significant differences

TABLE 4-1: KEY STEPS IN DEFINING PHENOMENA

Step	Description
1.Eliminate preconceived ideas; prevent errors	Clearlyspecifyitemstobeobservedinordertoavoid errorsbasedonsuppositionandrigidthinking
2.Observe on the shop floor	Tracetheproblembacktothesmallestpossibleunits bypersonallyobservingitsphysicalelementsatthe site
3.Classify phenomena	Adequatelyclassifywhatyouhaveobserved(5W1H)
4.Investigate deviations	Clarifythedistinctionbetweenwhatisnormaland abnormalinwhatyouhaveobserved

Using the 5Ws and 1H to stratify phenomena

An effective technique for defining phenomena is to use the questions Who, What, Where, When, Which, and How (5W + 1H) to stratify the results of observations. Table 4-2 provides an overview of this method.

TABLE 4-2: CLASSIFYING PHENOMENA WITH 5W + 1H

WHO	•Anyvariationamongpeopleinvolvedintheoperation? (Anymorning/day/nightshiftdifference?) (Anydifferencesamongnewoperators,floaters,temporarystaff?)
WHAT	•Anyvariationduetoproductionmaterials? (Anymaterialsdifferences?Differencesamonglots?) (Anyvariationduetodifferentpartdimensions,shapes?)
WHERE	•Anyvariationduetoequipment,fixtures,components? (Inwhatprocessandwhatmachineelementsdoestheproblem occur?) (Anydifferencesamongdifferentequipment,machinetypes?) (Anyvariationassociatedwithdifferentjigs,fixtures?)
WHEN	•Anyvariationrelatedtotimeorperiod? (Doestheproblemoccuratthestartofwork?Inthemiddle?) (Anytimedifferencesassociatedwithproblem?) (Anyseasonaldifferences?) (Duringwhichoperationsistheproblemapttooccur?) (Istheproblemlikelytooccuraftersetupchanges)
WHICH	•Arethereanycharacteristictrendsovertime? (Doproblemsincreaseordecrease?) (Anychangesbefore,after,orsimultaneously?)
HOW	•Anyvariationincircumstancesofoccurrence? (Doestheproblemoccurfrequentlyoronlyrarely?) (Doesitappearabruptlyorgradually?) (Doestheproblemappearcontinuouslyordiscontinuously?) (Doesitappearatregularorirregularintervals?)

Step 2: CONDUCT A PHYSICAL ANALYSIS

We introduced this step in Chapter 3 but review it in detail here in the context of the entire P-M analysis process. Physical analysis explains properly stratified phenomena from a physical point of view. Without physical analysis, we may judge factors by experience ("it's always been like that"), by intuition ("it must be like that"), or through impressions ("it's probably like that"). As a result, our action to correct chronic losses stops short of resolving the problem.

Think Visually

Some people may feel ill-equipped to express themselves in technical terms. But physical analysis does not require fancy words or complicated expressions. In fact, such words would only obscure the phenomenon. The best and simplest approach is to think visually. Consider drawing a diagram of how product and equipment elements interact to bring about the defect or functional failure.

Physical Analysis Procedure

Table 4-3 recaps the steps to be followed when analyzing phenomena in physical terms.

TABLE 4-3: KEY STEPS IN PHYSICAL ANALYSIS

Step	Description
1 Identify operating principles	Review machine diagrams and manuals to understand the equipment's basic operating principles
2 Identify operating standards	Learn the functions and mechanisms of equipment and devices by sketching simple machine diagrams
3 Identify interacting elements	Draw contact diagrams to identify what relationships define the phenomenon
4 Quantify the physical changes involved	Identify appropriate physical quantities and changes in those quantities

Physical analysis step 1: Identify operating principles
Before conducting P-M analysis, study the mechanical or physical principles underlying the operation in question. Identify and document those principles directly related to the phenomenon. It helps to diagram the structure of relevant mechanisms and show how they work.

Physical analysis step 2: Identify operating standards
Relate the operating principles to equipment mechanisms to identify standards that govern normal conditions. How do the mechanisms function when the abnormal phenomenon does not occur?

Table 4-4 shows examples of the operating principles and standards for defect-free operation.

TABLE 4-4: OPERATING PRINCIPLES AND STANDARDS IN MANUFACTURING PROCESSES

Operation	Operating Principle	Operating Standard
Lathe Cutting 	Turnchuckedworkpiece, applyingthecuttingtooltoits surface.Movecuttingtool paralleltotheworkpiece's rotationalaxistoremove materialfromitssurfaceuntil specifiedshapeanddimensions areobtained.	1. Turnworkpieceatthe specifiedRPMandcheckfor absenceofwobble. 2 Thecuttingtoolshouldalways moveinastraightline. 3. Makesureworkpiececenteris alignedwithtopedgeof cuttingtool.
Drilling 	Whiledrillisrotating,pressit (feedforward)toenablethedrill andchiseledgetoremove materialfromtheworkpieceand expelthematerialviathedrill grooves.Abandaroundthe drill'sperimeterprovidesahole guideandhelpsthedrill penetrateinastraightline.	1. Turnthedrillatthespecified RPMandcheckforabsence ofevennessandwobble. 2. Makesuredrill'scuttingedges arethesameshapeandsize allaround(checkdrilllength andangle). 3. Makesurethespindlemoves inastraightline.
Internal Grinding 	Usingtwoshoestosupportthe workpiece,turnitonthedrive plate.Turnthegrindstoneat highspeedandrepeatedlyapply ittotheworkpiecesurfaceuntil enoughofthesurfacehasbeen removedtoobtainthespecified shapeanddimensions.	1. Aligncenterofworkpiecewith centerofgrindstone. 2. Makesureoftheworkpiece rotationalcentersand grindstoneareparallel. 3. Makesuretheworkpieceand grindstonearebothturningat thespecifiedRPMandare freeofwobble. 4. Runonlyatthespecified cuttingspeed.
Arc Welding 	Createanarcinaninertgas betweenthebasematerialand theelectrodeandusetheheat ofthearctomeltandfuse(weld) thebasematerial.	1. Donotallowthecurrentto fluctuateduringwelding. 2. Maintainaconstantdistance betweentheelectrodeandthe basematerial. 3. Holdtheelectrodeatthe specifiedanglewhenmoving itforwardtoweldalongthe basematerial.
Rust	Whenoxygenandmetal combine,oxidation(rusting) occursinthemetal Example: $4Fe+3O_2 \longrightarrow 2Fe_2O_3$	

Physical analysis step 3: Identify interacting elements

Think of phenomena occurring in a manufacturing operation as cause-and-effect relationships between equipment and products. The "cause" aspect refers to the condition of the equipment and the "effect" is the quality of the product. Any deterioration of this relationship is necessarily reflected in product quality.

To explain this deterioration we consider the points of contact between the equipment and workpiece—the elements or equipment conditions that interact to produce the abnormal phenomenon. Contact diagrams such as those shown in Table 4-5 are effective tools for identifying interacting elements.

TABLE 4-5: INTERACTING ELEMENTS RELATED TO ABNORMAL PHENOMENA

Abnormal Phenomenon	Contact Diagram	Interacting Elements
Variability of OD dimension	center of rotation (A) — grindstone edge (B)	Workpiece center of rotation (A) and grindstone edge (B)
OD finish dimensions are conical	(B) spindle centers — (A)	Workpiece center (A) and axis of moving grindstone (B)

Physical analysis step 4: Quantify physical changes

Once the interacting elements have been identified and diagrammed, we need to quantify the physical changes that occur in their relationship, using basic physical units and/or constants. Table 4-6 shows the link between the phenomenon and quantifiable physical changes. Expressing the product-equipment relationship in measurable terms, it explains how this relationship changes when a malfunction occurs where:

A = the workpiece
B = the tool
C = the relationship (distance) between A and B, and
D = the change in relationship.

TABLE 4-6: ABNORMAL PHENOMENA AND QUANTIFIABLE CHANGE

Abnormal Phenomenon (contact diagram)	Interacting Elements	Quantitative Physical Changes
ODdimensionsfluctuate distance	Betweenworkpiece centerofrotation(A) andedgeofgrindstone (B)...	•distance(C) •fluctuates(D),so •finishdimensionsare notconstant
ODdimensionsbecomeconical distance	Betweenworkpiece centerofrotation(A) andaxisofmoving grindstone(B)...	•distance(C) •isnotparallel(D),so •cylindricityisnot achieved

The Importance of Understanding Equipment Mechanisms and Structure

Understanding the mechanisms and structure of the equipment involved is as important as defining the phenomenon. Intimate knowledge of the equipment helps clarify what happens to produce particular malfunctions or defects. "Mechanism" means a group of equipment elements with a single function and how it functions. "Structure" refers to how all the equipment elements are put together or assembled.

Do not omit this step. Conducting P-M analysis without understanding mechanisms and structure leads to gaps in the array of factors that may contribute to the problem. Bear in mind that we normally distinguish causal factors at three levels:

Causal Factors

- *Constituent conditions: all factors that account for the phenomenon*

- *Primary 4M correlations: all factors that account for each constituent condition*

- *Secondary 4M correlations: all factors that account for each primary 4M correlation*

When teams lack an adequate understanding of the machine, the gaps in their knowledge obscure the links between these levels and may cause them to overlook entire groups of factors. The inevitable result is an impressionistic P-M analysis.

The Value of Machine Diagrams

It is not easy to explain the mechanisms and structures of machines and devices, even when you use them every day. Therefore, it is especially useful to prepare machine diagrams when beginning P-M analysis. Drawing diagrams forces teams to examine carefully each part of the machine and often leads to the discovery of many hidden abnormalities. Contact diagrams (see Table 4-6) are also very helpful. Important aids in acquiring machine knowledge include the following:

- Read and reread the instruction manual until you understand it thoroughly.

- Prepare your own machine diagrams at the machine.

- Study process cycle, wiring, hydraulic, and any other system diagrams as well.

- Investigate setup and running conditions.

- Restore to normal any items out of specifications (do this before starting P-M analysis).

Sample Machine Diagram: Cylindrical Grinder

Figure 4-2 shows machine diagrams drawn up by an improvement team for a cylindrical grinder. Review the diagrams along with the following text description. When you can relate the process cycle to specific mechanisms depicted in the diagram, you have probably understood how the machine works.

In this example, conditions governing the workpiece (steadiness, work head precision, grinding parameters) are fixed.

Since conditions at the work head are fixed, let us consider the grindstone head mechanisms. These mechanisms can be broken down into three parts: (1) grindstone reconditioning, (2) compensatory feed, and (3) grinding.

Grindstone Reconditioning
The grindstone reconditioning mechanism reshapes the grinding wheel surface by "dressing" it (grinding it down) after a set number of pieces have been processed. The process begins when a hydraulic cylinder moves the reconditioning apparatus (dressing head) to the right and moves the end of the seesaw on the stylus. When the seesaw rides up on the right-hand stylus it turns to the left, causing the ratchet wheel to turn left as well.

FIGURE 4-2: CYLINDRICAL GRINDER DIAGRAMS

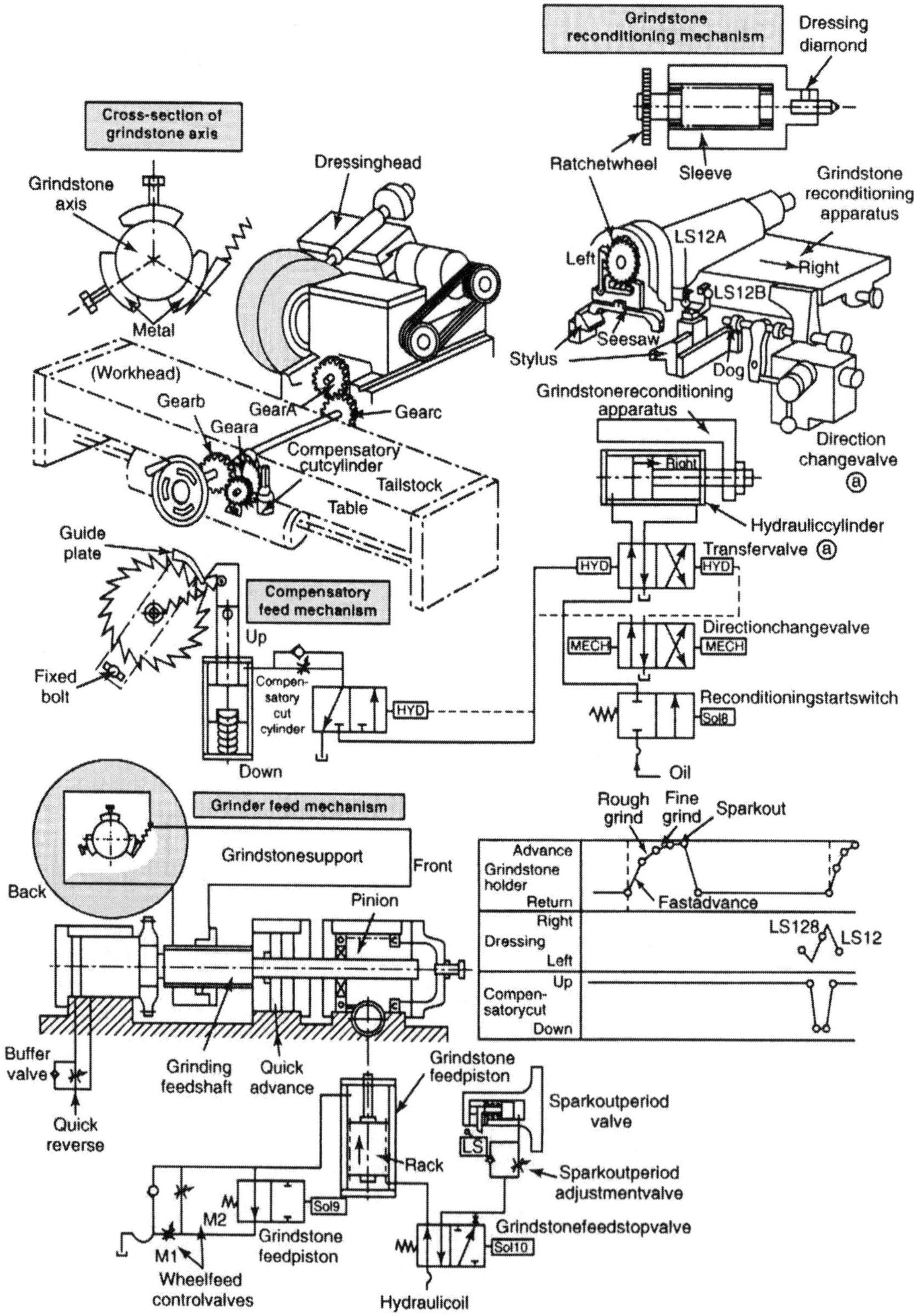

The ratchet wheel is attached to a male screw; its rotation causes the sleeve to advance by turning the female threads cut on the sleeve's interior diameter. By this mechanism, the dressing diamond mounted on the sleeve advances toward the center of the grindstone as dictated by the angle of ratchet wheel rotation. That distance constitutes the amount needed for one dressing pass (what it takes to regrind the worn grinding wheel).

Compensatory feed

Once the circumference of the grinding wheel has been reground, the wheel must be advanced by the amount removed by the dressing process. This is the function of the so-called "compensatory feed" mechanism.

First, dog A attached to the grindstone reconditioning apparatus moves to the right and pushes the lever on the direction change valve. This engages the ratchet wheel and causes it to rotate to the right. This turns gears *a, b, c,* and *A,* the last of which causes the grindstone feed spindle to turn and moves the grindstone forward (toward the workpiece).

Adjustment of the guide plate at this point can equalize the distance of forward travel by the dressing gear and the compensatory advance of the grindstone. In other words, loosening the fixed bolt of the guide plate and changing its angle makes it possible to adjust the amount by which the ratchet jaws slide. The amount of compensatory feed can be decreased as this slide distance increases.

Grinding

As the process cycle diagram shows, the grinding feed mechanism can change the speed at which the circumference of the part is cut after rapid advance. The sequence is rough grind (high cutting speed), fine grind (low cutting speed), then sparkout (zero cutting speed). Rapid advance that does not involve grinding is carried out by hydraulic pressure and the cylinder apparatus on the body of the grinding head.

Rough grinding. For rough grinding, hydraulic oil flows from the grindstone feed stop valve to the grindstone feed piston. Grinding speed is controlled by the grindstone feed transfer and wheel feed control (M1) valves at the exit of the piston. The exterior of the grindstone feed piston is a rack that protrudes from part of the cylinder and engages the pinion of the grindstone feed shaft. In other words, the advance of the piston causes the pinion to rotate, and that rotation of the male threads moves the grindstone forward.

Fine grinding. To slow down the rotation of the grindstone feed shaft's male threads for fine grinding, the grindstone feed transfer valve is closed by solenoid 9, and control of the grindstone feed piston's speed passes to the M2 wheel feed control valve. Valve M2 has a greater throttle range than valve M1, so the volume of oil escaping from the piston decreases and the grindstone advances more slowly.

Sparkout. Since grindstone speed is zero for sparkout operation, there is no need to supply hydraulic oil to the grindstone feed piston. Solenoid 10 moves the grindstone feed stop valve to the left and hydraulic oil flows through the sparkout period adjustment valve to the sparkout period valve. Changing the aperture of the sparkout period adjustment valve makes it possible to adjust the time until the limit switch is struck, which is the sparkout period.

Summary and Review of Physical Analysis

From a practical standpoint, seeing things in physical terms involves the following:

- From operating principles and standards, understand what elements (e.g., workpiece and tool) interact to define the phenomenon in question

- Determine how to measure the relationships between these elements in physical units (distance, temperature, speed, etc.)

- Understand how these relationships change with the phenomenon

- Display these relationships graphically

The Physical Analysis Process at Work

Figure 4-3 illustrates the process of physical analysis. In this example, note that we need to express the phenomenon clearly: not merely as an "OD finish defect," but as "variability in OD finish dimensions" or "OD finish conicality." This is important, because since different factors produce these two defects, different countermeasures will be needed to control each phenomenon.

FIGURE 4-3: THE PHYSICAL ANALYSIS PROCESS AT WORK

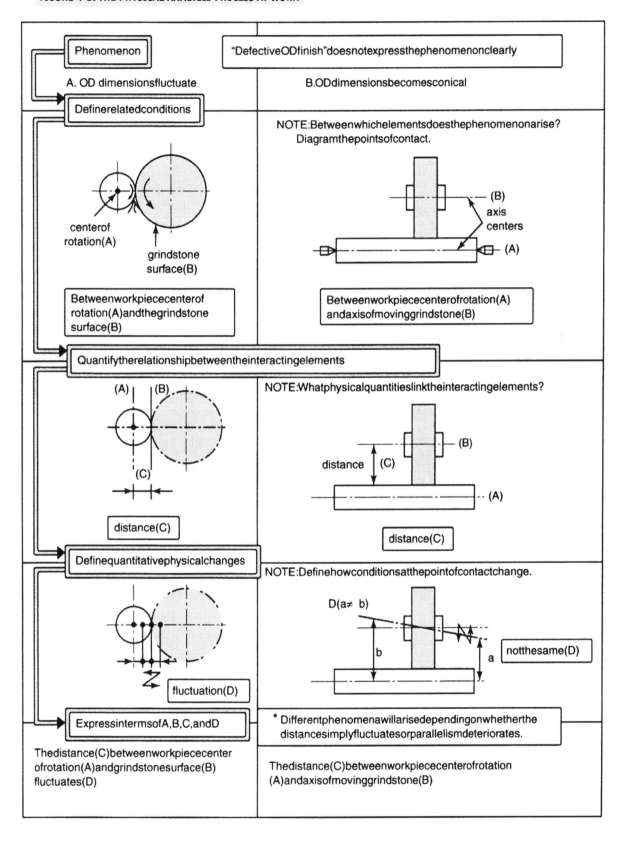

In this case, assume that the first two steps have already been accomplished, and that the team is ready to identify interacting elements and quantify physical changes. Following are the actual team activities needed to complete the physical analysis:

1. Diagram point-to-point and line-to-line relationships
First, draw the points of contact between equipment and workpiece to clarify the interacting elements. This reveals that variability in OD finish dimensions involves the workpiece center of rotation and the grinding point (the point of contact between the face of the grindstone and the circumference of the workpiece). Conicality of the OD dimensions arises from the relationship between the axial center of the workpiece and the axial center of the grindstone. The first step, then, is to express this relationship either on a diagram or in terms of the two axes, A and B.

2. Quantify the relationship between elements in contact
Review the physical quantity or quantities linking the elements. The relevant physical quantity in this example might be the relative positions of A and B, that is, the *distance* separating them.

3. Clarify changes in the physical quantity
Clarify how the physical quantity changes. In this case, the phenomenon appears different (abnormal) precisely because the distance between the elements has changed.

The preceding can be summarized through either the final diagram or a written explanation of how the physical quantity C linking objects A and B changes by the amount D. For example, "the distance C between the workpiece center of rotation A and the grindstone face B fluctuates by D." Either representation constitutes a physical analysis of the phenomenon. As you can see, contact diagrams play an extremely important role in the analytical process. Often, a physical analysis that is hard to express in words can be represented in a diagram.

What to Do When Physical Analysis Isn't Working

When this approach fails to yield a physical analysis, go back and review the phenomenon for inadequate stratification. Two or more phenomena were probably bound together as one. Inadequate stratification is also likely if there seems to be more than one physical analysis, since we established earlier that there can only be one per phenomenon.

Step 3: IDENTIFY CONSTITUENT CONDITIONS

The next step is to review all the conditions that consistently give rise to the problem. These are the *constituent conditions* either necessary or sufficient for the physical phenomenon analyzed in the previous step to occur. It is important to consider everything that might conceivably bring about ("constitute") the phenomenon, regardless of preconceived ideas or intuitive judgments. These conditions encompass all causal factors, so this step ensures that no such factors are overlooked.

As shown in Table 4-7, any constituent condition falls into one of the 4M categories of production inputs:

- Machines: equipment function and precision

- Man (People): the level of human skills

- Materials: quality of parts/materials leaving the previous process

- Methods: appropriateness of procedures and standards

These categories are useful in P-M analysis because defect phenomena can always be traced back to causal factors in at least one of the four areas.

TABLE 4-7: CONSTITUENT CONDITIONS

4M Category	Constituent Conditions
Equipment precision and reliability	Whenever any part of a machine malfunctions, check for links with abnormal phenomena and for the conditions that give rise to those phenomena
Methods and Standards	Check for links with physical defect phenomena whenever designated standards are inadequate or too lax
People quality of applied skills	Check for links with abnormal phenomena when people charged with adhering to standards do not do so
Material quality from previous processes	Check for links with abnormal phenomena when materials or parts from previous processes are of poor quality

Steps for Reviewing Constituent Conditions

The steps shown in Table 4-8 are helpful when checking each of the 4Ms to see whether off-standard conditions may be linked to defect phenomena. Table 4-9 provides a simple example of the approach. Constituent conditions 1 through 5 concern equipment precision. In other words, when any of these five mechanical elements does not function properly, quality defects result. Items 6 and 7 are examples concerning methods and materials, respectively. The phenomenon may be linked to standards that are inadequate, too loose, or simply ignored (item 6), or problems with the material supplied (item 7).

TABLE 4-8: PROCEDURE FOR CHECKING CONSTITUENT CONDITIONS

Step	Description
1. Identify equipment mechanisms	Identify the functional units which constitute the equipment
2. Understand how mechanisms function together	Examine each mechanism and identify the role it plays in relation to the equipment as a whole
3. Consider the cause-and-effect relationship between mechanisms and abnormal phenomena	Check for links with abnormal phenomena when any mechanism, subassembly, or component fails to play its expected role
4. Identify constituent equipment conditions	Investigate links between the appearance of abnormal phenomena and the condition of mechanisms potentially connected to such phenomena
5. Identify constituent conditions related to standards and to people charged with adhering to them	Even if equipment mechanisms are fulfilling their expected roles, check to see if abnormal phenomena appear when (a) designated standards are too lax or inadequate or (b) people charged with adhering to those standards are not doing so
6. Identify constituent conditions related to the quality of previous processes	Even if conditions involving the equipment, standards, and people's adherence are all in order, check for physical defect phenomena resulting from quality defects in incoming material

TABLE 4-9: CHECKING FOR CONSTITUENT CONDITIONS

Phenomenon: OD dimensions fluctuate to both sides of specifications

Physical Analysis	Constituent Conditions
Finishingdimensionsareunstablebecauseof fluctuations(D)indistance(C)between workpiececenterofrotation(A)andedgeof grindstone(B) (A)(B) → ← (C)	1.Theworkpiececenterofrotation fluctuates.
	2.Thepositionoftheleadinggrindstone edgefluctuates.
	3.Theamountremovedduringdressing fluctuates.
	4.Theamountremovedincutting correctionsfluctuates.
	5.Thecuttingmotioncycleofthegrinder headfluctuates.
	6.Somestandardsareinadequateornot followed.
	7.Qualityfrompreviousprocessis unstable.

Key Points

In reviewing conditions that give rise to physical defect phenomena, consider the following:

1. Understand that constituent conditions are identified by reviewing correlations with the elements of production known as the 4Ms (equipment, people, material, method).

2. Review and understand equipment mechanisms and structure before trying to identify constituent conditions.

3. Determine the state each functional element must be in to generate the abnormal phenomenon: note off-standard conditions within each element.

4. Confirm that each of these conditions helps bring about the phenomenon.

5. Go back through the 4M correlations to make sure no other conditions have been overlooked.

STUDY 4Ms FOR CAUSAL FACTORS

List and investigate any correlations between the constituent conditions identified in the previous step and the basic production inputs or 4Ms (equipment, people, materials, methods). Put another way, this means identifying cause-and-effect relationships between constituent conditions and specific 4M elements. The constituent condition becomes the "effect," and we review 4M elements for potential "causes." Identify all logically conceivable elements necessary to generate the constituent conditions.

Primary and Secondary 4M Correlations

As we mentioned in Chapter 3, there are three levels of factors, starting with constituent conditions. The terms *primary 4M correlation* and *secondary 4M correlation* refer to these next two levels. This is shown in Figure 4-4. The constituent conditions are identified at the mechanism level. Primary and secondary correlations step down to the subassembly and component levels, respectively. (A *mechanism* consists of related physical elements with a single function. The machine elements of the mechanism are *subassemblies* made up in turn of *components*.) Of course the number of levels can vary; for instance, you may have four or five in the case of more complex machines.

FIGURE 4-4: THE THREE LEVELS OF CAUSAL FACTORS

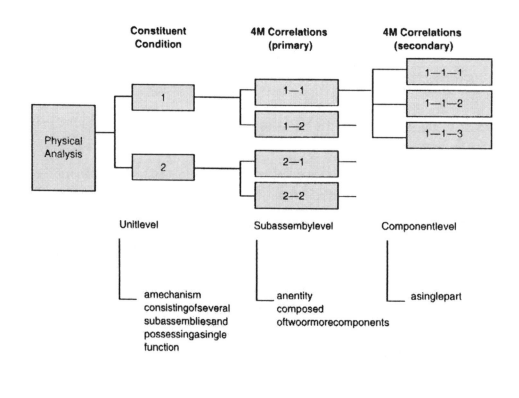

Correlations should express cause-and-effect relations

Figure 4-5 shows the correlative relationships between constituent conditions and the production inputs (4Ms). If the constituent condition is the effect, the primary 4Ms are causes. Similarly, secondary 4Ms are the causes of primary 4M "effects." Note that primary 4M items must lead to constituent conditions. At each step, in other words, only cause-and-effect relations may be represented.

For a clearer picture of the cause-and-effect relationship among these three levels of factors, consider this simple example:

- **Phenomenon:** A car's engine will not start.

- **Constituent Conditions (mechanism level):**
  1. Gasoline is not supplied to the engine.
  2. Electrical power is not supplied to the engine.

- **Primary 4Ms (subassembly level):**
  1-1. The fuel system is without gasoline.
  2-1. The battery is without power.

- **Secondary 4Ms (component level):**
  1-1-1. The gasket between the gas tank and the fuel lines is worn.
  1-1-2. The gas tank is empty.
  2-1-1. A battery cable is loose.
  2-1-2. The battery is dead.

FIGURE 4-5: THE CAUSE-AND-EFFECT CHAIN LINKING THE THREE FACTOR LEVELS

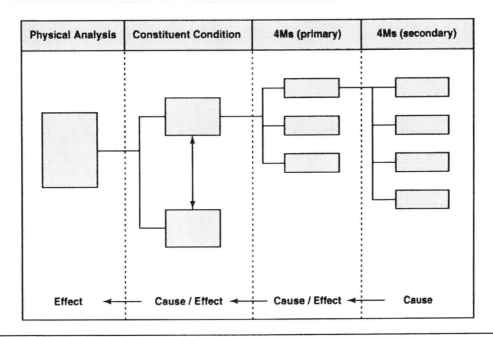

Express 4M elements in measurable terms

Constituent conditions and both primary and secondary correlations are all potential causes we may want to address through various countermeasures. Therefore, 4M elements should be expressed in measurable (verifiable) terms as much as possible. Otherwise, there is no way to make evaluative judgments and set standard values. In the primary 4M stage, one occasionally encounters a phrase such as "part mounted poorly"—a vague description difficult to evaluate or relate to any standard. A better designation might be "workpiece alignment is out of square with the reference plate."

Key Points in Deriving Primary 4M Correlations

Consider the following key issues when identifying primary 4M correlations with production inputs:

1. Ignore contributory degree or extent of impact. In P-M analysis we set prioritization aside.

2. When assessing correlations with equipment, tools, or dies, work progressively within subassembly units, from the mechanism's functional tip or surface (the "processing point") to the base that supports it.

3. List all logically conceivable items for material (precision of earlier processes), method (including run, setup, measurement, and operating methods), and human elements (skills), as well as for machines and equipment.

4. Review primary correlations list to confirm that they actually result in the constituent conditions.

Table 4-10 gives an example of primary production input analysis.

Key Points in Deriving Secondary 4M Correlations

Here again it is important to list all factors regardless of impact or degree of involvement. Take each primary correlation and reduce it to its constituent elements (in this case, the component level). For each secondary correlation identified, ask whether it actually contributes to a corresponding primary factor. This is the same procedure used at the primary 4M stage. Table 4-11 is an example of secondary 4M analysis.

TABLE 4-10: SAMPLE 4M CORRELATIONS (PRIMARY)

Physical Analysis	Constituent Conditions	Primary 4M Correlations
Thedistancebetweenthe workpiececenterofrotation andthecuttingtoolvaries oneithersideofspecified values(±)	1.Thepositionofthecuttingtoolvaries(±) conventionallathe	1-1 Cuttingtoolmoves 1-2 Toolpostholderwobbles 1-3 Toolpostwobbles 1-4 Crossslidewobbles 1-5 Carriagewobbles

TABLE 4-11: SAMPLE 4M CORRELATIONS (SECONDARY)

Constituent Conditions	Primary 4M Correlations	Secondary 4M Correlations
1.Positionofcutting toolvaries(±)	1-1 Cuttingtool moves	1-1-1 Loosetoolclampingbolts 1-1-2 Toolnotrigidenough 1-1-3 Hardwareirregularities
2.Amountof grindstonetaken offduringdressing varies	2-1 Feeddistanceof diamonddresser varies	2-1-1 Wornfeedscrew 2-1-2 Loosebearingsupportingdiamond dressershaft 2-1-3 Loosefixationboltsupportingdiamond dressershaft 2-1-4 Worndiamond
3.Cutcompensation varies	3-1 Numberof compensatory cutsvaries	3-1-1 Loosedogondirectionchangevalve 3-1-2 Wornlocatorpinondirectionchange valve 3-1-3 Wornballondirectionchangevalve 3-1-4 Slackspringholdingdownball

Steps 1 Through 4 Illustrated

Step 4 concludes the "front end" of P-M analysis: starting with the phenomenon and progressing logically to identification of all causal factors. (Under the conventional approach, many teams jump straight to this point, with incomplete results.)

We can summarize these first four steps with a simple example. Consider a malfunctioning piston rod. Step 1 clarifies that the rod sometimes stops in mid-stroke within the air cylinder (this is the phenomenon). In Step 2 our physical analysis explains that the resistance received by the rod is greater than its advancing force. We identify two conditions during Step 3 that might bring about the phenomenon:

Constituent Conditions

1. *The driving force of the rod is low.*

2. *Resistance received by the rod is high.*

Then in Step 4 we investigate possible causes for each of these conditions at the levels of primary and secondary 4M correlation.

Primary 4M Correlations for Conditions 1 and 2

1-1 Air is not reaching the piston
1-2 Air is leaking inside the cylinder

2-1 There is resistance between the piston rod and rod cover
2-2 There is resistance between the piston and the cylinder tube
2-3 Exhaust air remains

For each primary correlation we look for secondary correlations. Here are secondary correlations for primary correlations 1–1 and 1–2 only:

1-1 Air is not reaching the piston:

1-1-1   *Low air pressure*
1-1-2   *Ripped air hose*
1-1-3   *Air hose too long*
1-1-4   *Air hose bent*
1-1-5   *Excessive drainage accumulation*
1-1-6   *Foreign matter clogging joint*
1-1-7   *Air leak through joint*

1-2 Air is leaking inside the cylinder:

1-2-1   *Piston packing blemish or wear*
1-2-2   *Piston gasket blemish or wear*
1-2-3   *Cushion packing blemish or wear*
1-2-4   *Rod packing blemish or wear*
1-2-5   *O-ring blemish or wear*
1-2-6   *Cylinder gasket blemish or wear*
1-2-7   *Bushing blemish or wear*
1-2-8   *Rod cover blemish or crack*
1-2-9   *Cylinder tube blemish or rip*
1-2-10   *Piston packing mounted in reverse*
1-2-11   *Piston gasket mounted in reverse*
1-2-12   *Head cover packing mounted in reverse*
1-2-13   *Rod cover packing mounted in reverse*

This detailed analysis is continued for each primary correlation.

Step 4 produces a *complete* list of causal factors. This approach is certainly more thorough and effective than randomly guessing about operator error, lack of lubrication, and so on.

P-M Analysis—The Full Cause-and-Effect Chain

Before proceeding to the next step, it may help to look briefly at the larger picture. Figure 4-6 summarizes the full chain of cause-and-effect relationships examined in P-M analysis:

- Abnormal phenomena are understood and physically analyzed at the mechanism level to identify constituent conditions (Steps 1 through 3).

- Constituent conditions are analyzed according to the 4Ms at the subassembly level to identify primary correlations (Step 4).

- Primary correlations are analyzed according to the 4Ms at the component level to identify secondary correlations (Step 4).

Once all potential causes have been identified, we are ready to move toward solutions. After taking a hard second look at factors needing control to ensure we have not overlooked any abnormalities, we plan and conduct activities designed to restore or improve the equipment (Steps 7 and 8).

FIGURE 4-6: THE FULL CAUSE-AND-EFFECT CHAIN IN P-M ANALYSIS

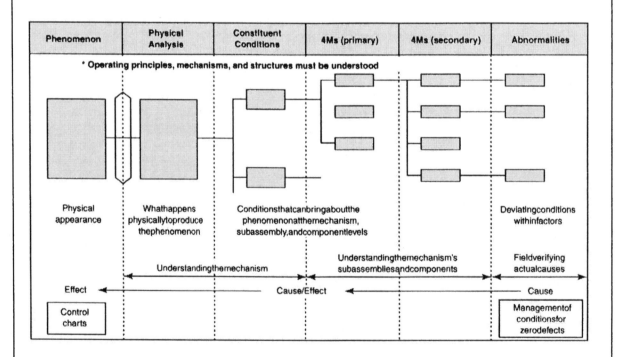

ESTABLISH OPTIMAL CONDITIONS (STANDARD VALUES)

Steps 1 through 4 have defined the defect phenomenon, analyzed it in physical terms, and then listed all factors conceivably linked to it at three levels: mechanisms, subassemblies, and components. Now we need to seek out and identify all abnormalities (including the slightest) within these factors.

Objective Basis for Identifying Abnormalities

Consistent with the P-M analysis philosophy, this search cannot be entrusted to mere subjective judgments. The team should establish reliable criteria for determining whether each potential cause listed is normal or abnormal. In other words, what conditions, if present, will prevent this problem from recurring?

Review Existing Standards

Begin by surveying the standards and criteria already established for controlling this stage of the production process.[1] If no suitable criteria exist for evaluating equipment precision, develop and institute new ones that reflect operating principles, the mechanics of defect and malfunction generation, equipment function and structure, and product quality.

Table 4-12 suggests various sources of 4M-related standards for optimal conditions as well as criteria for their development. Most processes already involve numerous standards, criteria, or other norms. However, when different departments have responsibility for such standards they are often overlooked or ignored. Therefore, it is important to go back to the beginning and review and evaluate these standards.

---

1. *Do not confuse this step with Step 2 of physical analysis, "Identify Operating Standards." The difference lies in point of application. In physical analysis "operating standards" help us clarify the mechanics of abnormal phenomena—the* effect. *This step helps us identify what is abnormal in each factor that constitutes a* cause.

TABLE 4-12: 4M STANDARDS AND NORMS

4Ms	Standards, Norms, and Criteria
Equipment precision	1. Find normal values from equipment diagrams and operating instructions 2. Find normal values from equipment inspection records 3. Find normal values from daily check standards and periodic maintenance criteria 4. Set standards based on correlations among equipment functions, design, and quality standards. Note: Check previously established standards for accuracy on the same basis
Previous process quality	1. Use quality criteria to clearly identify characteristics that must be guaranteed at previous processes. Note: Make sure that quality standards are comprehensive
Level of standards	1. Examine and understand current task standards for equipment setup and operation, assembly, and inspection. Note: Make sure existing task standards are accurate
Human skills	1. Clearly identify what is involved in adhering to such standards

Determine the Boundaries between Normal and Abnormal

When establishing criteria, consider carefully where to locate boundaries between what is normal and what is not. The dividing line can be difficult to place in gray areas between normal and abnormal. There is, however, a high probability that phenomena in this boundary area are linked to defect generation. So try to eliminate uncertainty from the decision whenever possible. Figure 4-7 suggests more than one way to accomplish this:

- Where there is already a clear dividing line, shift it to narrow the normal range (taking a conservative approach to make sure no abnormal conditions slip in).

- Where there is a "gray area," fix it to a line toward the normal side, or at least narrow the range.

Key Points for Establishing Optimal Conditions

It is worth recalling a definition from Chapter 1: Optimal = Necessary + Desirable. The way things *should be*, not the way they *have been*. Setting standards for optimal conditions, therefore, means setting them for zero defects.

FIGURE 4-7: THE BOUNDARY BETWEEN NORMAL AND ABNORMAL

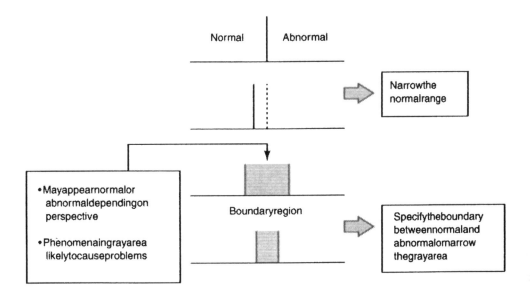

If there are no standards or if those in place are of doubtful value, conduct analyses or experiments to establish or confirm them. If necessary, set provisional standards, implement them on a trial-and-error basis, and then check the results. In any case, remember that the standards serve the process (and not vice versa), so try to maintain optimal conditions through a variety of strategies while you look for the most appropriate standards to assure them. Moreover, while you search, work to improve actual conditions on the shop floor.

Establishing Optimal Conditions

1. *Return to square one and study all relevant standards.*

2. *Do not take existing standards at face value; look at how functions and structure relate to quality standards and study each relevant manual to determine the true optimal conditions.*

3. *Clarify the boundary between normal and abnormal.*

4. *Do not give up when there are no existing standards; confirm instead via analyses and experiments.*

5. *As you search for appropriate standards for optimal conditions, keep working to improve actual conditions while maintaining those standards.*

Step 6: SURVEY CAUSAL FACTORS FOR ABNORMALITIES

In this step teams do the following:

1. Determine the most reliable, efficient ways to measure the gap between the condition of causal factors identified in Steps 3 and 4 and their ideal values confirmed in Step 5.

2. Determine the most efficient way to physically survey all the factors at the machine location.

3. Conduct the survey, measuring targeted values and comparing them to optimal standards to determine which factors contain abnormalities and thus are actual causes of the defect phenomenon.

Select Appropriate Methods

No one person is familiar with all the methods that may be required to measure these various factors. To avoid administrative and maintenance problems later, bring in qualified people from other departments to help select the most appropriate methods. Table 4-13 lists some approaches that may apply.

Plan for the Best Use of Your Time

When reviewing how measurements should be made, start with the constituent conditions. This reduces the number of survey items, which in turn saves employee-hours. If some constituent conditions are found to be free of abnormalities, there is no need to measure and review their primary and secondary 4M correlations.[2]

Reviewing measurement methods speeds up the improvement process and also clarifies the preventive maintenance tasks that will keep abnormal conditions from recurring.

---

2. In such cases, teams may jump straight from Step 3 to Steps 5 and 6 for those items, then return to Step 4 for conditions that require further investigation.

TABLE 4-13: MEASUREMENT UNITS AND MEASURING DEVICES

No.	Item Measured	Measurement Tool	No.	Item Measured	Measurement Tool
1	Axlelooseness	Dialgauge,smalltest	25	Innerdiameter measurement	Cylindergauge,airmicrometer
2	Edgewobble	Dialgauge,smalltest	26	Roundness	Roundnessmeter
3	Linearity	Autocollimator	27	Cylindricality	Lengthmeasuringmachine
4	Flatness	Autocollimator,laser-mediated flatnessgauge	28	Surfaceroughness	Surfaceroughnessgauge
			29	Cutsurf acechatter	High-resolutionroughnessgauge
5	Orthogonality	Lasercoordinatemeasuring machine	30	Abrasion	Dimensiongauge
			31	Hardness	Hardnessgauge
6	Cyclelinedrawing	Visigraph	32	Surfacehardness (forthinitems)	Superficialhardnessgauge
7	Belttension	Tensionmeter	33	Fit	Blue
8	Looseness	Dialgauge,springbalance	34	Residual stress	X-rayresidualstressmeter
9	Vibration	Vibrationanalyzer,FFT	35	Residual magnetism	Gaussometer
10	RPM	Tachometer,vibrotester	36	Grindingcrack	Acidbathtest,hydrochloricacid macrotest
11	Rotational abnormalities	Vibrotester			
12	Grindstonebalance	Vibrotester	37	Backlash	Thicknessgauge
13	Frequency	Oscilloscope	38	Gearmesh	Gearmeshtester
14	Loadcurrent	Ammeter,penrecorder	39	Angle	Anglegauge,autocollimator, rotaryencoder
15	Power	Wattmeter			
16	Resistance	Insulationtester	40	Hydraulicfluid contamination	Automaticmicroscopicparticle counter
17	Temperature	Thermometer	41	Coolant contamination	Millipore
18	Temperature distribution	Radiationthermometer (thermotracer)	42	pH	pHmeter,chemicalanalysis
			43	Aircleanliness	Particlecounter
19	Warping	Warpmeter	44	Sound	Noisemeter,FFT
20	Boltfastening strength	Torquewrench	45	Brightness	Illuminationmeter
21	Torque	Torquemeter	46	Flowrate	Flowmeter
22	Force	Loadscale,springforcemeter	47	Horizontallevel	Levelgauge
23	Pressure	Pressureguage, micropressuregauge	48	Linecentering	Pianowire
24	Outside(major) diameter	Micrometer,dialgauge	49	Ingredients, composition	X-raymicroanalyzer, electronmicroscope

Keys to Reviewing Measurement and Survey Methods

1. *Review the measurement and survey methods, starting with the constituent conditions (if these are normal, you need not study primary and secondary 4Ms)*

2. *Plan the survey*
   - When: *date, shift, duration*
   - Who *does* what: *responsibilities assigned to various departments and individuals*
   - *With* what: *organize the setup with work tools, measuring instruments*

Conducting the Survey

Ideally, teams should survey all items listed as causal factors. However, this is usually too time-consuming to be practical. As implied above, the procedure can be streamlined by taking it one level at a time:

1. Measure the status of all items listed as constituent conditions. (If these are normal, skip the 4M correlations.)

2. Review and measure primary 4Ms only for constituent conditions whose measured values are different from the standard values (use temporary standards if necessary).

3. Review and measure secondary 4Ms only for the primary 4Ms whose measured values are different from the standard values.

DETERMINE ABNORMALITIES TO BE ADDRESSED

Now that we have identified all causal factors and surveyed their condition using appropriate measurement methods, we are ready to decide which deviating conditions will be considered true abnormalities and treated. The following guidelines may prove helpful:

Keys to Identifying Abnormalities

1. *Thoroughly investigate all factors*

2. *Compare abnormal conditions against current or provisional standards*

3. *Think in terms of optimal conditions, not just necessary conditions*

4. *Classify as abnormal any items on the border between normal and abnormal*

5. *Make sure you understand the causal factors behind each condition classified as abnormal*

Think in Terms of Optimal Conditions

For items with current standards, compare the actual conditions with the standards and classify as abnormal all items that are off-standard. When doing this, do not limit your thinking to old concepts and criteria about what constitutes "normal" vs. "abnormal." Instead, imagine what the original, defect-free conditions would have been and watch for even the slightest abnormality. We will emphasize it one more time—the standard is how things "should be," not "have been."

Classify All Borderline Conditions as Abnormal

At the review stage, people often stop investigating factors as soon as they find one or two abnormalities that appear to have a big impact on the results. To achieve zero chronic loss, however, teams must investigate all selected factors thoroughly. Chronic loss often arises from "borderline" conditions—items that appear normal from one perspective and abnormal from another. Classify all such borderline items as abnormal.

Focus on Prevention

While these abnormalities represent one end of the cause-and-effect chain for the purposes of P-M analysis, they too should be viewed as effects with causes of their own. Rather than address each item at face value, always ask "why did this happen?" and "what factors caused this to happen?" When planning improvements, remember that the ultimate goal is to restore conditions to their original state.

To do this, teams must thoroughly review the causal factors in selected abnormalities with an eye toward prevention. For example, if a defect involves the presence of dirt or dust, ask what allowed the contamination. Plan improvements that not only correct the causes but also prevent their recurrence so that zero chronic defects can be maintained.

Step 8: PROPOSE AND MAKE IMPROVEMENTS

In this eighth and final P-M analysis step, teams propose and make any corrections and improvements required for each abnormality, then plan and institute appropriate preventive measures. Note the following points:

Keys to Implementing Improvements

1. *Remember that restoration (to optimal conditions) comes before replacement or design modification.*

2. *After restoration, plan improvements that solve hardware problems, update obsolete technologies, and prevent recurrence.*

3. *In restoring and improving equipment, group as many factors as possible and handle them together.*

4. *Confirm the accuracy of all results. Ask, "have any factors been left out?" and "are the standard values correct?"*

5. *Standardize improvements and institute preventive measures to prevent backsliding.*

Restore before Improving Equipment

When dealing with chronic abnormalities, it is natural to speculate about how the equipment or process might be modified or improved. When defective conditions are ignored, however, the results often remain unsatisfactory no matter which mechanisms are replaced or which part-shapes or materials are changed. So, restore the original, defect-free conditions before considering design modifications or replacements. If after carefully restoring these conditions the results are still inadequate, then begin thinking about modifications.

Address *All* Causal Factors

Chronic defects that become the focus of P-M analysis often have a combination of causes. There will be many factors whose cause-and-effect relationships are not understood. Teams cannot expect satisfactory results, however, by acting only upon those causes that appear to have a major impact. Restore and, if necessary, make improvements for *all* the selected causal factors. Try this comprehensive approach just once and you will see its power.

If after restoring and improving all factors your results are still unsatisfactory, consider two possible reasons. Either some factors were omitted or the standard values are too lenient. When this happens, the only recourse is to "go back to the drawing board" and conduct another P-M analysis.

Standardize

Last, but not least important, is standardization. Be sure to implement preventive measures and add or revise operating standards as needed to maintain optimal conditions. Only when abnormalities no longer occur or when you can detect their early signs and correct them can you say that the job of eliminating them is finished.

TABLE 4-14: KEYS TO CONDUCTING P-M ANALYSIS

1. The P-M analysis team should include at least four members: preferably an operator, a supervisor, a maintenance technician, and a manufacturing engineer.

2. Enhance P-M analysis charts with simple drawings or sketches (to clarify obscure terminology or complex expressions).

3. List all causal factors, regardless of magnitude or apparent impact.

4. After P-M analysis is complete, be sure to review it for clarity and completeness. For one, check for links in the cause-and-effect chain (from secondary to primary 4M correlations to constituent conditions).

5. If the standard values for a causal factor are unclear, use temporary values and establish standards after reviewing the results.

6. For greater efficiency, conduct onsite surveys for P-M analysis in the following sequence:
   • Survey constituent conditions and determine which are abnormal
   • Survey only those primary 4Ms that correlate to abnormal constituent conditions (marked with an "x")
   • Survey only those secondary 4Ms that correlate to abnormal primary 4Ms

7. Group the abnormalities you have identified and correct them together.

8. Thoroughly restoring original (nondefective) conditions takes priority over making improvements.

9. Continually ask "why" about each abnormality and pursue potential causes among all the 4Ms, including human behavior.

10. When P-M analysis results are disappointing, either some factors have been omitted or the standard values are too lenient. In either case, you must carry out P-M analysis again.

11. Enter variable and semivariable factors into preventive maintenance checklists to ensure proper management of conditions.

12. Check up on the process to make sure decisions are being carried out as intended.

13. P-M analysis is less a method than a way of thinking about things. Everyone from the shop floor to manufacturing managers should give this approach a closer look. It only takes two or three experiences applying P-M analysis to see what a difference it makes!

KEYS TO CONDUCTING P-M ANALYSIS

Table 4-14 summarizes key guidelines and tips for conducting P-M analysis. In addition, consider the following check items for best results.

Is the Conceptual Process Correct?

☐ Did you correctly stratify and identify the phenomena?
☐ Did you do a correct physical analysis of the phenomena?
☐ Did you study all the constituent conditions?
☐ Did you study all the relevant drawings, such as machine, component configuration, and component function drawings?
☐ Did you make a complete and logical list of causal factors?
☐ Did you make logical connections among the physical analysis, constituent conditions, and primary and secondary correlations?

Are Abnormality Measurement Processes Correct?

☐ Did you use correct measurement methods to expose abnormalities?
☐ Did you classify the abnormalities correctly?
☐ Did you include slight defects?
☐ Are the standard values current and correct?
☐ Are the pass/fail criteria satisfactory?

Are Results Satisfactory?

☐ Were countermeasures implemented for all abnormalities?
☐ Were all countermeasures successful?
☐ Were all countermeasures with unsatisfactory results repeated (to discover other causal factors and defects)?

No P-M analysis can be truly successful unless the analyses are logical and defect identification and measurement processes are carried out correctly.

Usually results are not good because abnormalities are overlooked or faulty defect measurement has caused some abnormalities to be omitted. In some cases, however, teams get good results even when their processes are flawed. Sheer luck permits them to find and eliminate some causal factors and defects behind the problem. In such cases, absence of true understanding often results in temporary solutions only; the improved conditions cannot be maintained for long.

P-M Analysis in Action

THIS CHAPTER EXAMINES the "nuts and bolts" of P-M analysis through an example of its application at a plant that manufactures hydraulic solenoid valves.

BACKGROUND OF PROBLEM (HYDRAULIC SOLENOID VALVE DEFECTS)

As shown in Figure 5-1, the hydraulic solenoid valve consists of a body, spool, coil, and movable iron core. Two common problems with this type of solenoid valve are (1) vibration and noise if the core is not fitted precisely and (2) coil burnout.

FIGURE 5-1: STRUCTURE OF HYDRAULIC SOLENOID VALVE

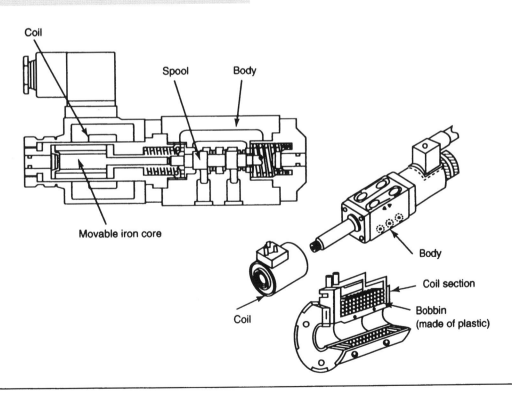

In many cases, such malfunctions are caused by accumulated dirt in the spool (which interferes with valve operation) rather than by a steady decrease in suction. Although malfunctions are seldom caused by coil failures, the manufactured quality of the coil does affect solenoid longevity. So at this plant all coils are fully inspected.

This company set a goal of cutting defects by half, and formed a project team at the plant to carry out improvements. They were also building a TPM program, and had decided to include P-M analysis as one of their problem-solving tools.

P-M Step 1: | CLARIFY THE PHENOMENON

The project team recognized the need to first define the defect phenomena occurring in the plant.

To clearly define phenomena related to shop floor problems, we ask *why* over and over. As we look at how the team stepped through this simple technique, we can better understand how it works.

Why Do Quality Defects Occur at This Plant?

One way to answer this question is to categorize defects by type. The project team decided to first look at quality defects by part. The main parts machined at this factory are those same four mentioned earlier—valve bodies, spools, coils, and movable iron cores. The team found that 41 percent of all process defects were in the coil (Figure 5-2).

FIGURE 5-2: PARETO DIAGRAM OF PROCESS DEFECTS

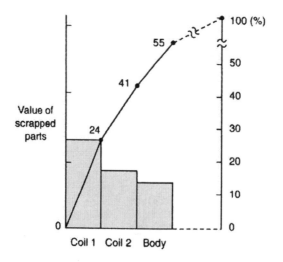

Why Do Coil Defects Occur?

The coil manufacturing process is outlined in Figure 5-3. The defective coils are discovered at final inspection. While many items are inspected at this point, we can see that 60 percent of all coil defects are due to "voltage test defects." This means in turn that about 25 percent (0.60 times 0.41) of all hydraulic solenoid valve defects stem from voltage test (electrical) defects in the coils.

FIGURE 5-3: DEFECTS IN COIL MANUFACTURING PROCESS

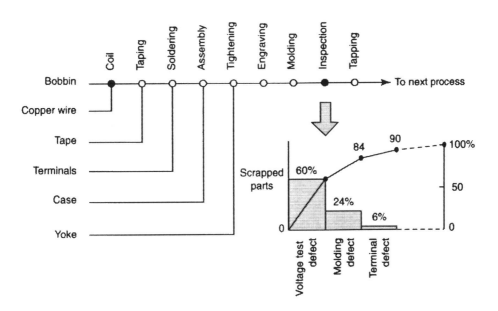

Why Do Voltage Test Defects Occur?

As illustrated in Figure 5-4, the voltage test checks for even the slightest current leakage into the yoke and coil case when a 2,000-volt AC charge is passed through to the coil for two seconds. If current leaks into either of these elements, it will also leak into the valve body. The standards for the body are zero current and at least 100 megaohms insulation resistance.

FIGURE 5-4: HOW THE VOLTAGE TEST WORKS

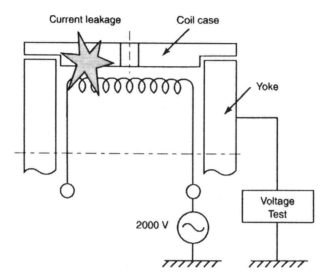

When the project team members took apart one of the coils that had failed the voltage test, they found traces of current leakage between the coil and coil case. Because the copper wire had been wrapped around a plastic bobbin (similar to those used for the lower thread in sewing machines), there was adequate insulation between the yoke and the coil. However, the insulation between the coil and the case was merely a small gap. They surmised this gap had something to do with the voltage test defect.

Why Do Gap Width Changes Occur?

Next, they studied how the copper wire was wrapped around the bobbin and found the coil to be thicker in some places than in others (Figure 5-5). They checked these differences with a dimension gauge and found that in some specimens the gap was a mere 0.2 mm (Figure 5-6).

FIGURE 5-5: COIL THICKNESS VARIATION

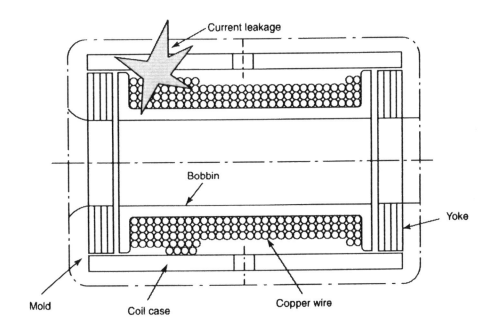

Current leakage

Bobbin

Yoke

Mold

Coil case

Copper wire

FIGURE 5-6: PROFILE OF COIL WITH VOLTAGE TEST DEFECT

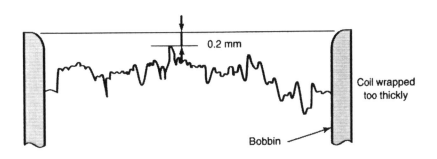

0.2 mm

Coil wrapped
too thickly

Bobbin

By answering these four simple *why* questions, the project team learned that about 25 percent of their process defects were tied to voltage test defects in coils, and that their top priority was to reduce coil thickness variation. They went straight to work planning for improvement. To summarize this line of questioning:

1. Why do quality defects occur? Because many of the coils are defective.

2. Why do coil defects occur? Because many voltage test defects are found at the final inspection.

3. Why do voltage test defects occur? Because of changes in gap width between the coil and coil case.

4. Why do gap width changes occur? Because there is variation in the coil winding thickness (irregular winding).

Through this technique, the project team defined the phenomenon clearly enough to see that voltage test defects could actually be reduced to zero. Since the problem was due to irregular coil winding, the obvious solution was to make sure the coils were wound regularly.

Phenomenon

Variation in coil winding thickness

P-M Step 2: | CONDUCT A PHYSICAL ANALYSIS

Analyzing the phenomenon in physical terms means using physical principles to define the interaction—the points of contact—between equipment and product. These reflect what we called the equipment's *operating principles* in Chapters 3 and 4. In this case, the phenomenon is that the coil gets wound too thickly in places. How did the project team define the interacting elements for this phenomenon?

Physical Analysis = Illustrating the Interaction between Equipment and Product

First, the project team made a contact diagram (Figure 5-7). The contact point at the coil winding process is between the flyer and the bobbin, since these are the two elements that wind the copper wire. Looking at this illustration and thinking in terms of operating principles, the next

FIGURE 5-7: CONTACT DIAGRAM FOR THE COIL WINDING PROCESS

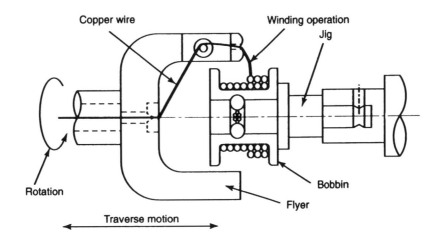

step was to clarify how the flyer rotates while also moving laterally, both at constant speeds, to wind a consistent length and thickness of copper wire around the bobbin.

Define the Phenomenon in Terms of Operating Principles

Refer to Figure 5-7 again. Thickness variation in coil winding occurs when the coil is wound too many times (in other words, has too many layers) in the same place. In other words, one wire would be on top of another when it should have been directly beside it, making the coil thicker at that point.

At this stage, it helps to set aside technical terms such as "operating principles" and instead just consider what you *see*. One of the team members drew a second contact diagram (Figure 5-8) and in studying it wondered if any variation existed in the intervals between wires. The project team discussed it and arrived at the physical analysis, "variation in the pitch (lateral distance) per rotation as the flyer winds the copper wire around the bobbin." This is a logical description of the phenomenon.

Physical Analysis

Variation in the pitch per rotation as the flyer winds the copper wire around the bobbin

FIGURE 5-8: PHYSICAL ANALYSIS ILLUSTRATED

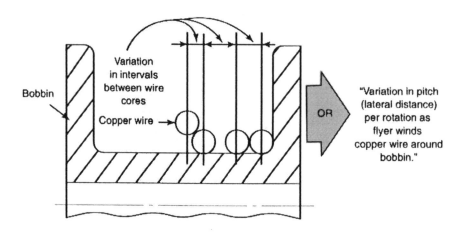

P-M Step 3: IDENTIFY CONSTITUENT CONDITIONS

Equipped with this physical analysis of the phenomenon, the team next sought to identify the conditions that consistently bring it about.

That meant looking at the operating principle—"the flyer both rotates and moves laterally as the copper wire is wound around the bobbin"—and asking which condition(s) must change to create the phenomenon—"variation in the pitch per rotation as the flyer winds the copper wire around the bobbin." Drawing simple illustrations of the equipment mechanisms helped the team study these *constituent conditions*.

Study the Coil Winding Equipment and Its Mechanisms

Remember from our earlier chapters that P-M analysis identifies causal factors at three levels. The first is the *mechanism* level, and those factors are called constituent conditions. Once the phenomenon has been analyzed in terms of equipment-product interaction, attention shifts to the equipment mechanisms involved in this interaction.

This coil winding process uses a small numerically controlled turntable winder (the equipment). As shown in Figure 5-9, it consists of four main units: a tensioner, a drive mechanism, a winder, and an index table. Let us look at each of these mechanisms and their respective functions:

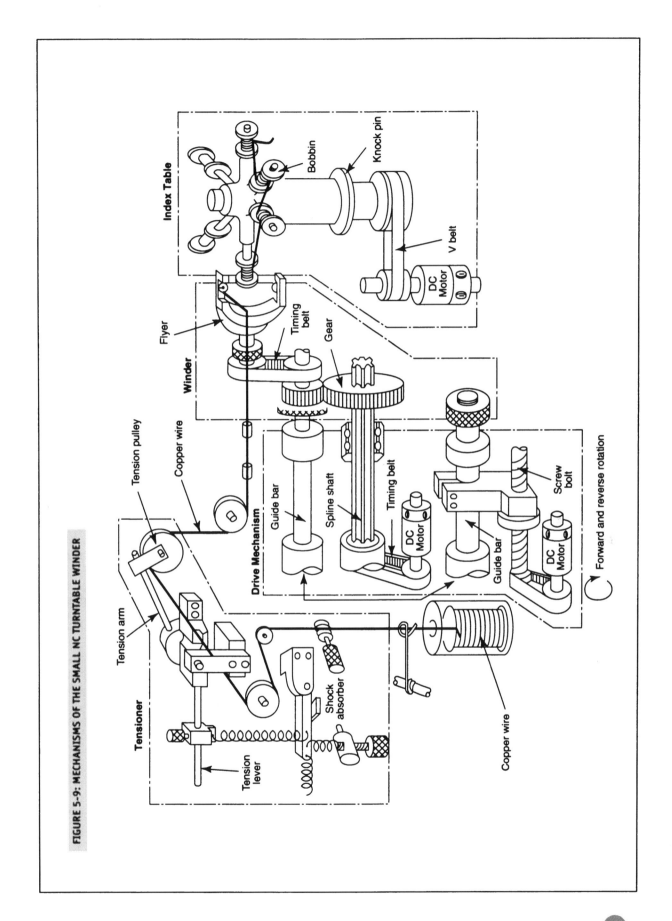

FIGURE 5-9: MECHANISMS OF THE SMALL NC TURNTABLE WINDER

Index Table

Bobbin

Knock pin

V belt

DC Motor

Flyer

Timing belt

Winder

Gear

Tensioner

Tension pulley

Copper wire

Tension arm

Tension lever

Shock absorber

Drive Mechanism

Guide bar

Spline shaft

Timing belt

DC Motor

Screw bolt

Guide bar

DC Motor

Forward and reverse rotation

Copper wire

Tensioner

The tensioner supplies the copper wire to the bobbin at constant tension. The wire is pulled from its case, then through a guide hole and set of guide pulleys to reach the tensioner. From there it passes through a hole in the center of the flyer and then through a guide hole at the edge of one of the flyer arms. The motion of the slide base attached to the tension lever applies tension according to wire thickness, then uses tension arm flexion (much like a fishing pole) to maintain it. In addition, a shock absorber attached below reduces any shocks received from the winder.

Drive mechanism

The drive mechanism and winder act as a single unit with two functions: (1) maintaining flyer traverse motion and (2) maintaining flyer rotation, both at constant speed. The drive mechanism includes two drive shafts, one screw bolt, and one spline shaft. It runs two DC motors with input from an NC control panel. The lower DC motor turns a timing belt which rotates the screw bolt. The upper part of the female screw is attached to a guide bar, and the rotation of the screw bolt causes the guide bar to move laterally. Meanwhile, the upper DC motor turns another timing belt which rotates the spline shaft.

Winder

The winder is anchored by a nut to one end of the guide bar that extends from the drive mechanism. The flyer picks up its traverse motion from the guide bar and its rotation from the spline shaft (through a set of gears and another timing belt). Looking back at the drive mechanism and winder together, we can say that one motor moves the flyer back and forth while the other keeps it rotating.

Index table

The index table moves the bobbins to their correct positions and holds them there. It has six jigs, each holding a bobbin. A third DC motor turns the index table and a knock pin ensures that the jigs stop in the specified positions when the table is rotated.

Principal Mechanisms and Their Functions

1. *Tensioner:* maintains correct tension in the wire

2. *Drive mechanism & winder:* maintain the flyer's traverse motion at standard speed

3. *Drive mechanism & winder:* maintain the flyer's rotation at standard speed

4. *Index table:* maintains the bobbins in their correct positions

---

Sort Out the Constituent Conditions for the Copper Wire Pitch Variation

Having examined the small turntable winder mechanisms and their functions, we are now ready to sort out constituent conditions. The assumption here is that *something in at least one of the mechanisms is interfering with its normal function,* and that voltage test defects are occurring as a result.

Remember that the project team identified the defect phenomenon as "variation in coil winding thickness" and physically analyzed it as "variation in copper wire pitch." We want to know which mechanisms contain the cause of this problem. Let's organize our analysis as follows:

Constituent Conditions (by Mechanism)

1. ***Tensioner:*** *variation in tension could cause variation in copper wire pitch*

2. ***Drive mechanism and winder:*** *variation in the flyer's traverse speed could cause variation in copper wire pitch*

3. ***Drive mechanism and winder:*** *variation in the flyer's rotational speed could cause variation in copper wire pitch*

4. ***Index table:*** *variation in bobbin position could cause variation in copper wire pitch*

These are the constituent conditions from the perspective of one of the 4Ms, the manufacturing equipment ("machine"), materials, methods, and people ("man") should also be considered. The voltage test defects could be tied to incoming quality defects, in turn due to faulty work methods or defective materials at a previous process. Also, the setup for the coil winding process is carried out by an operator. Consequently, there are two more constituent conditions:

---

5. ***Quality defects*** *from a previous process could cause variation in copper wire pitch*

6. ***Improper methods*** *in the coil winding process could cause variation in copper wire pitch*

Table 5-1 summarizes the P-M analysis steps taken so far.

TABLE 5-1: P-M ANALYSIS UP THROUGH STEP 3 (IDENTIFY CONSTITUENT CONDITIONS)

Clarify the Phenomenon	Conduct a Physical Analysis (make drawings while thinking)	Identify Constituent Conditions (for mechanisms, materials, people, methods)
Coll thickness variation	 Variation here Variation in the pitch (lateral distance) per rotation as the flyer winds copper wire around the bobbin	1. Tension on copper wire varies 2. Traverse speed of flyer varies (left to right) 3. Flyer rotation speed varies 4. Bobbin position moves 5. Defect in materials from previous process 6. Improper work methods

SET OPTIMAL CONDITIONS; SURVEY FACTORS

After reviewing constituent conditions, a team would normally proceed to Step 4, "Study 4Ms for Causal Factors," which involves reviewing the 4Ms at the subassembly and component levels for each condition. P-M analysis can be a time-consuming process, however, so to maximize its efficiency without sacrificing effectiveness, Step 4 may be skipped to advance directly to Step 5. This is done to verify which constituent conditions contain actual causes. Then the team can study primary and secondary 4Ms for those conditions only. The project team chose this route.

Review Maintenance Check Items, Measurement Methods, and Standard Values

Studying the role of each mechanism helps identify constituent conditions. To evaluate the equipment's operation at this level, teams should review the precision and maintenance checks, measurement methods, and standard values for these same mechanisms.

Find a way to measure each condition

The project team had a difficult time determining how to quantify "tension variation." However, they knew that omitting this measure could prevent them from controlling the constituent conditions later on. So they began by searching for a good way to measure tension.

One team member consulted with an outside supplier of measurement instruments who agreed to rent them a tension meter designed specifically for their purpose.

Set or revise standard values as needed

Before team members could review the maintenance check items and measurement methods, they had to solve another difficult problem. No standard values for tension or pitch existed. The team worked out the correct pitch values by extrapolating from RPM settings for the two DC motors and for each wire thickness, but a set of correct tension values was an altogether different problem.

Without any standard values for tension they never had any means of measuring it. Likewise, the work standards did not explain how to make tension measurements. Team members ultimately constructed a table of standard data from correct tension values found in the equipment operation manual.

Review the Actual Condition of the Machine in Operation

Table 5-2 shows the results of the on-site survey comparing constituent conditions to standard values.

TABLE 5-2: SURVEY OF CONSTITUENT CONDITIONS

Check Site	Check Items (for condition control)	Measurement Methods (Illustrated)	Standard Values	Measured Value	Evaluation
Tensioner	Tension variation	Use tension meter / Copper wire / Tension meter	Example: 0.32 510-580g	120-580g	Improvement required
Winder and drive mechanism	Variation in traverse speed	Check for variation in traverse positions	Traverse origin ± 0.03 mm	±0.02 mm	OK
			Return point ± 0.05 mm	max. 0.32 mm	Improvement required
	Variation in rotational speed (RPM)	Check for variation in RPM / Tachometer	Within ± 2%	0%	OK
Index table	Variation in bobbin position	Use dial gauge	± 0.05 mm	max. 0.29 mm	Improvement required
Quality at previous process for materials	Check bobbins' dimensional precision	Use digital calipers	Under study (no existing standard)	Large variation	Improvement required
	Variation in copper wire thickness	Micrometer	± 0.003 mm	± 0.006 mm	Further study required
Work methods	Method for setting correct tension	Check work standards and methods		No table of correct tension values	Improvement required
	Method for setting correct pitch	Check work standards and methods		No table of correct pitch values	Establish table of correct pitch values

P-M Step 4: STUDY 4Ms FOR CAUSAL FACTORS

All constituent conditions deviating from their correct values should at this point be checked for 4M correlations with the aid of mechanism drawings.

While both the review of survey methods and the survey itself could be done with the equipment running, investigation of 4M correlations within any mechanism requires some downtime. It is therefore important at this stage to list *all* causal factors imaginable before going out to the shop floor. That way everything can be checked during one shutdown.

Table 5-3, which is a P-M analysis table, lists all the causal factors from Steps 3 and 4. Note that only three of the six constituent conditions were studied, since the others had fallen within specified tolerances and were thus no longer suspect. The time saved by measuring each condition before reviewing 4M correlations underscores how important planning is in making improvement activities as efficient as possible.

P-M Steps 7–8: IDENTIFY ABNORMALITIES; MAKE IMPROVEMENTS

Once team members had completed the list of causal factors, their next step was to shut down the equipment and complete an internal inspection based on this list. They approached this inspection knowing what abnormalities to look for, and also knowing these abnormalities would inevitably occur. At the same time, the team also realized that careful, sustained attention would be necessary to find them all.

This kind of mental preparation is critical. Our natural tendency is to keep thinking "no problem so far" and consequently overlook potential causes. The P-M analysis table is one aid in preventing such oversights.

TABLE 5-3: P-M ANALYSIS TABLE

Phenomenon: Variation in coil thickness
Physical Analysis: Variation in the pitch (lateral distance) per rotation
as flyer winds copper wire around bobbin

Constituent Conditions	Primary 4M Correlations	Secondary 4M Correlations
1. Variation in tension	1-1 Tension setting outside rated values	1-1-1 Loose spring anchor block 1-1-2 Loose block anchor bolt 1-1-3 Spring fatigue 1-1-4 Loose shock absorber plate 1-1-5 Shock absorber spring fatigue 1-1-6 Loose shock absorber spring adjustment bolt 1-1-7 Loose tension lever anchor 1-1-8 Loose tension arm anchor bolt
	1-2 Cannot maintain tension	1-2-1 Defective winding of copper wire onto supply wheel 1-2-2 Worn rubber tensioner 1-2-3 Loose tensioner adjustment bolt 1-2-4 Defective rotation in one or more pulleys 1-2-5 Contamination or clogging of one or more guide holes 1-2-6 Misalignment of guide hole and guide rollers 1-2-7 Defective tension arm materials 1-2-8 Deterioration of arm flexion 1-2-9 Loose arm anchor 1-2-10 Defective flyer rotation
2. Variation in traverse speed (lateral motion)	2-1 Change in DC motor RPM	2-1-1 Defective control signal 2-1-2 Defect in DC motor control 2-1-3 Deterioration in DC motor mechanisms
	2-2 Change in screw bolt RPM	2-2-1 Loose or worn timing belt 2-2-2 Worn timing pulley 2-2-3 Loose pulley 2-2-4 Loose bearing
	2-3 Change in flyer edge speed	2-3-1 Worn screw bolt 2-3-2 Loose block anchor bolt 2-3-3 Worn or damaged guide bar 2-3-4 Worn or loose slide bearing 2-3-5 Loose winder fastening nuts 2-3-6 Loose flyer fastening nuts 2-3-7 Worn or damaged flyer spindle 2-3-8 Backlash or looseness in gear(s) 2-3-9 Loose or damaged timing belt 2-3-10 Worn or loose timing pulley
3. Change in RPM	No problems	
4. Variation in bobbin position	4-1 Bobbin position set imprecisely	4-1-1 Defective DC motor control 4-1-2 Worn or damaged V belt 4-1-3 Worn or damaged V pulley 4-1-4 Worn or loose knock pin 4-1-5 Worn or damaged knock hole
	4-2 Movement of index table	4-2-1 Worn or damaged slide surface 4-2-2 Index head angles set incorrectly
	4-3 Movement of bobbin	4-3-1 Loose jig (or wear or damage) 4-3-2 Incorrect gap between jig and bobbin 4-3-3 Stabilizing spring fatigue 4-3-4 Worn or damaged stabilizing holes
5. Defective materials from previous process	Survey completed	
6. Poor work methods	Survey completed	

Table 5-4 lists all abnormalities the team identified after surveying each causal factor, along with results of corrective actions and improvements. As you can see, these measures centered on three themes: (1) stabilizing the tension, (2) stabilizing the traverse positions, and (3) ensuring precise bobbin positioning. Among the abnormalities addressed were commonly overlooked items such as dirty rollers, clogged guide holes, and loose timing belts. Clearly, one intangible side benefit of P-M analysis for this team was increased awareness of equipment defects, including the slightest ones.

TABLE 5-4: REVIEW OF SURVEY RESULTS

Check Site	Check Item	Measurement Method	Standard Values	Measured Values	Evaluation	Restoration/Improvement	Result
Tensioner	Tension variation	Tension meter	φ 0.32 510 ~ 580 g	120 ~ 580 g	Action required	1 Remodeled tensioner 2 Cleaned all rollers 3 Cleaned all guide holes	Confirmed within rated values
Winder and drive mechanism	Variation in traverse speed	Dial gauge	Origin ± 0.03 mm	± 0.02 mm	OK	OK	OK
			Return point ± 0.05 mm	Max. 0.32 mm	Action required	1 Tightened loose timing belt 2 Programmed a half-second stop at the return point	Confirmed within 0.03 mm
	Variation in RPM	Tachometer	± 2%	0%	OK	OK	OK
Index table	Variation in bobbin position	Dial gauge	± 0.05 mm	Max. 0.29 mm	Action required	1 Made turntable level 2 Restored jig precision	Under study
Quality of material from previous process	Bobbin dimensional precision	Digital calipers	Under study		Action required	Asked manufacturer to fix mold	
	Variation in wire thickness	Micrometer	± 0.003 mm	± 0.006 mm	?	Outside manufacturer's standards; under discussion	
Work methods	Method for setting correct tension	Check work standards and methods		No table of correct tension values	Table must be established	Correct tension for each wire width is in the equipment operation manual	
	Method for setting correct pitch	Check work standards and methods		No table of correct pitch values	Table must be established	Correct flyer traverse speed and RPM for each wire width are in the equipment operation manual	

Confirm Results and Take Steps to Prevent Recurrence

Step 8 of P-M analysis actually consists of two phases: first proposing and making improvements to *attain* optimal conditions, then verifying the improvements' effectiveness and instituting standards and preventive measures to *maintain* optimal conditions. When the initial action fails to correct the abnormality, another round of improvements must be initiated until one of them works.

Figure 5-10 reflects coil thickness measurements taken after all improvements to the tensioner mechanism were in place. A dimension gauge was used to measure the copper wire wound onto the bobbins.

FIGURE 5-10: PROFILE OF COIL AFTER IMPROVEMENT

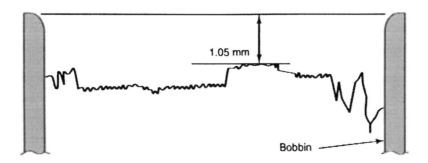

Compare these measurements with the same ones taken before improvement, as shown in Figure 5-6. In Figure 5-10, the large variations in coil thickness are gone, and the coil is wound much more evenly. Now the gap between coil and case is never less than 1.05 mm. This "extra" space was made not through some new technology, but simply by eliminating the coil bulges due to irregular winding.

Note also in Figure 5-11 that as expected, the improvements that eliminated coil thickness variation effectively reduced voltage test defects to zero. Even more importantly for the long term, these successful improvements proved to people in the plant that they can achieve "zero defects."

FIGURE 5-11: REDUCTION IN VOLTAGE TEST DEFECTS

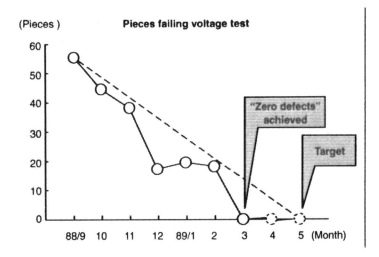

To make sure these gains would not be short-lived, the manufacturing engineering staff added a number of autonomous maintenance procedures for the small NC turntable winder, including cleaning all rollers and guide holes and adjusting the timing belts. They also added "check copper wire tension" to the setup tasks in the retooling manual and implemented other standardization measures to prevent backsliding and maintain zero defects.

P-M Analysis Practice

THE FOLLOWING P-M ANALYSIS PRACTICE EXERCISE is carried out by participants in P-M analysis seminars conducted by the Japan Institute of Plant Maintenance in Japan. You can do this exercise at home or with team members, or use it as a model for developing your own exercise.

Exercise Instructions

1. Assemble a plastic model of a four-wheel drive all-terrain vehicle (ATV) like the one shown in Figure 6-1. (The reader need not do this, of course. In the seminar, ATV models were actually assembled by groups of participants and a race was held later in the classroom.)

2. Make a drawing of its mechanisms. (Again, instead of doing this, just review the drawing shown in Figure 6-2.)

3. Carry out a P-M analysis (physical analysis, constituent conditions, primary and secondary 4M correlations) using blank forms patterned after Tables 6-1 and 6-2 on pp. 104 and 105.

In this case, use as your defect phenomenon "After power is switched on, the motor turns over a little but then dies." Please carry out the analysis as far as secondary 4M correlations. Table 6-3 shows the actual response from one of the participant groups.

FIGURE 6-1: ATV MODEL (SIDE VIEW)

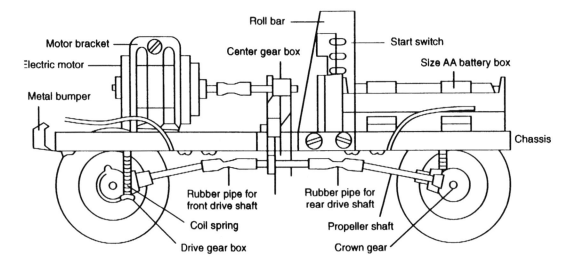

FIGURE 6-2: ATV MECHANISMS

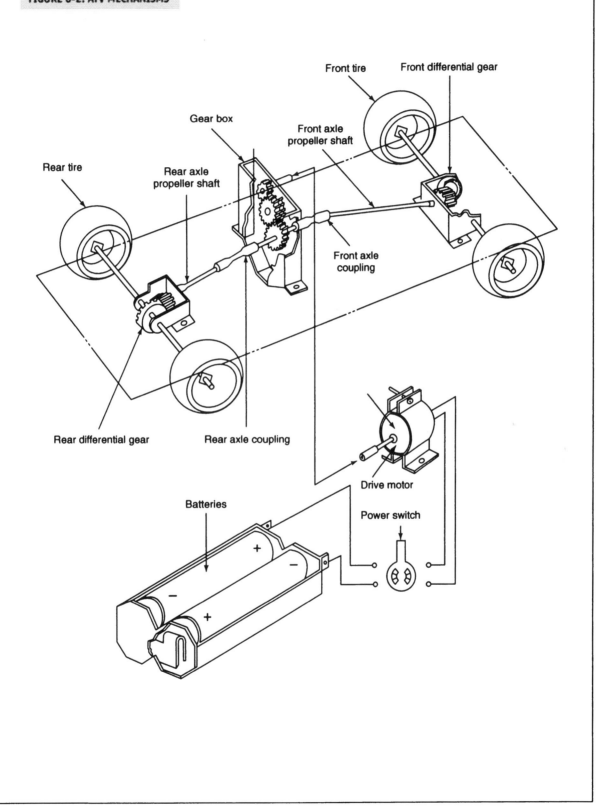

Front tire
Front differential gear
Gear box
Front axle
propeller shaft
Rear tire
Rear axle
propeller shaft
Front axle
coupling
Rear differential gear
Rear axle coupling
Drive motor
Batteries
Power switch

TABLE 6-1: P-M ANALYSIS FORM

P-M ANALYSIS FORM

Process: _____

Equipment: _____

Quality Characteristics: _____

_____

_____

Current Status: _____

Phenomenon: _____

Date: _____

Preparer: _____

Section head: _____

Manager: _____

Foreman: _____

Special notes: _____

Physical Analysis	Constituent Conditions		Primary 4M Correlations		Secondary 4M Correlations	
	Items (must be illustrated)	Standard Values	Items (must be illustrated)	Standard Values	Items (must be illustrated)	Standard Values

TABLE 6-2: SURVEY RESULTS FORM

SURVEY RESULTS FORM

Process: _____

Equipment: _____

Quality Characteristics: _____
_____

Current Status: _____
_____

Phenomenon: _____

Date: _____

Preparer: _____

Section head: _____

Manager: _____

Foreman: _____

Special notes: _____
_____

Check Site (mechanism)	Check Items (for condition control)	Condition Settings		Measurement Method (must be illustrated)	Survey Findings		Evaluation	Actions	Results
		Standard Values	Quality Impact		Measured Values	Quality Impact			

TABLE 6-3: SAMPLE P-M ANALYSIS RESPONSE (ATV EXERCISE)

Process: _____

Equipment: _____

Quality Characteristics: _____

_____

_____

Current Status: _____

Date: _____

Preparer: _____

Section head: _____

Manager: _____

Foreman: _____

Special notes: _____

Phenomenon: After power is switched on, the motor turns over a little, but then dies.

Physical Analysis	Constituent Conditions		Primary 4M Correlations		Secondary 4M Correlations	
	Items (must be illustrated)	Standard Values	Items (must be illustrated)	Standard Values	Items (must be illustrated)	Standard Values
The motor applies more torque to the front wheels than the rear wheels { Drive system load is too much for the motor torque	1 Motor torque output is less than the standard value		1-1 Not enough voltage applied to motor		1-1-1 Battery voltage is low 1-1-2 Defective contact between batteries and metal contact points in battery box 1-1-3 Defective contact between metal contact points in battery box and reverse switch 1-1-4 Defective contact point within reverse switch 1-1-5 Defective contact point between reverse switch terminal and cord 1-1-6 Defective contact point between motor terminal and cord	
			1-2 Underpowered motor		1-2-1 Worn motor brush 1-2-2 Defective coil insulation 1-2-3 Galled or worn motor bearing 1-2-4 Bent or loose motor bearing	
	2 Drive system load is too great		2-1 Motor output shaft and center gear input shaft are off center		2-1-1 Loose motor mounts 2-1-2 Loose motor bracket mount 2-1-3 Adjustment error when tightening motor bracket mount 2-1-4 Loose center gear box mount	

Physical Analysis	Constituent Conditions		Primary 4M Correlations		Secondary 4M Correlations	
	Items (must be illustrated)	Standard Values	Items (must be illustrated)	Standard Values	Items (must be illustrated)	Standard Values
			2-2 Too much rotary resistance inside center gear box		2-2-1 Worn or damaged gear(s) 2-2-2 Irregular pitch among gear shafts 2-2-3 Dirt or debris caught in gear mesh 2-2-4 Bent gear shaft 2-2-5 Galled or worn gear bearing 2-2-6 Bent or twisted gear box	
			2-3 Slippage between center gear box output shaft and propeller shaft centers (front and back)		2-3-1 Loose bolt in center gear box 2-3-2 Wheels out of alignment due to uneven tightening of drive gear box mounts	
			2-4 Too much rotary resistance inside drive gear boxes (front and back)		2-4-1 Worn or damaged gear 2-4-2 Poor mesh between pinion gear and crown gear 2-4-3 Dirt or debris caught in gear gear mesh 2-4-4 Galled or worn pinion gear bearing 2-4-5 Galled or worn crown gear bearing 2-4-6 Galled or worn axle bearing 2-4-7 Bent axle 2-4-8 Bent propeller shaft	
			2-5 Contact between tire and chassis		2-5-1 Loose tire nut 2-5-2 Axle out of alignment 2-5-3 Bent axle 2-5-4 Tire installed in wrong position	
			2-6 Contact between tire and fender		2-6-1 Axle out of alignment 2-6-2 Fender installed in wrong position	
			2-7 Contact between tire and bumper		2-7-1 Missing bolt in bumper 2-7-2 Bumper installed in wrong position	

COMMON ERRORS AND CORRECTED EXAMPLES

Table 6-4 displays a team response to a similar exercise from another P-M analysis seminar along with instructor corrections. In this case, the phenomenon was "Deviation in relative positions of workpiece center and 5.9 drill hole position." The errors and corrections are summarized as follows:

Errors and Corrections

1. Error in physical analysis: *"Workpiece center and hole center do not match"*

- *This is a restatement of the phenomenon and not a true physical analysis.*
- *A physical analysis could be "Deviation in relative positions of center of workpiece and center of drill rotation."*

2. More illustrations needed

- *Contact diagrams should clearly illustrate the relations between the workpiece, table, jig, guide bushing, drill, spindle, and other items.*
- *Illustrations of the spindle structure, slide surface, bushing mounting method, and other aspects of the problem would also be helpful.*

3. Error in listing of primary 4M correlations

- *Some factors were overlooked, such as the change in table centering (which should be listed whether the change is evident or not).*
- *Only the main spindle is addressed; usually, there should be at least two primary correlations listed.*

4. Error in listing of primary 4M correlations
- *Some factors were overlooked; for example the lower spindle center on the drill stand is not vertical.*
- *The drill bit is the only item addressed; normally, at least two primary correlations should be listed.*

5. Error in listing of secondary 4M correlations
- *Insufficient bearing lubrication has no direct relation to the main spindle center change.*
- *Technically, the main spindle's eccentric wear should be listed as a tertiary rather than a secondary factor.*

6. Error in listing of secondary 4M correlations
- *Internal guide bushing wear has no direct relation to looseness in the same.*
- *This item should be listed as a primary correlation item.*

7. Error in listing of secondary 4M correlations
- *Poor quality bushing material has no direct relation to guide bushing looseness (but could be listed as a tertiary factor behind internal bushing wear or looseness in the bushing case).*
- *If a relation is evident, guide bushing looseness should be described more specifically.*

8. Error in listing of secondary 4M correlations
- *Outer diameter of small guide bushing has no direct relation to looseness of drill bit bushing.*

TABLE 6–4: SAMPLE P-M ANALYSIS FORM WITH CORRECTIONS

Table 6-2. Sample P-M Analysis Form with Corrections

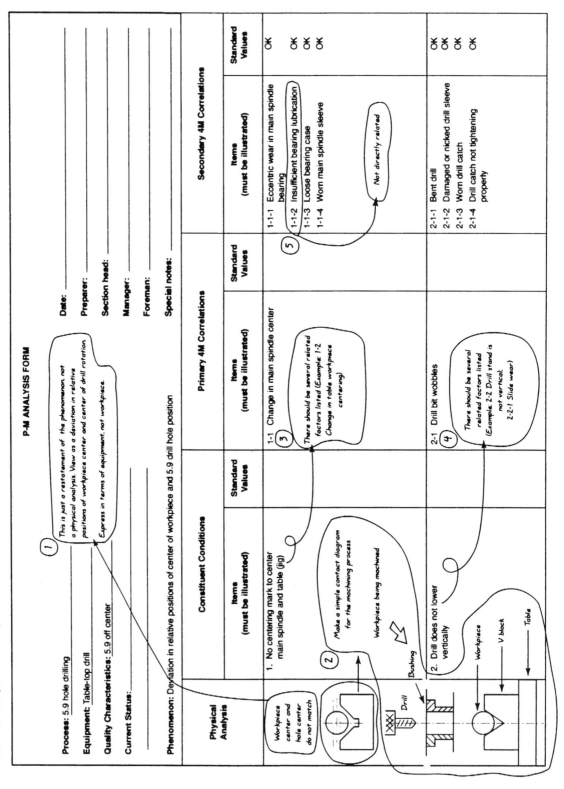

Table 6-2. P-M Analysis Form, cont'd

Phenomenon: Deviation in relative positions of center of workpiece and 5.9 drill hole position

Physical Analysis	Constituent Conditions		Primary 4M Correlations		Secondary 4M Correlations	
	Items (must be illustrated)	Standard Values	Items (must be illustrated)	Standard Values	Items (must be illustrated)	Standard Values
Workpiece center and hole center do not match	3. Variation in drill tip and workpiece drill point		3-1 Loose drill guide bushing		3-1-1 Internal wear in guide bushing	X
			φ 5.9 guide bush		3-1-2 Loose guide bushing case	OK
			3-2 Internal wear in guide bushing (formerly 3-1-1)		3-1-3 Guide bushing outer diameter too small	OK
					3-1-4 Guide bushing made of poor-quality material	△
			3-2 Change in workpiece clamping pressure		3-2-1 Insufficient pressurizer lubrication	OK
			⑦ Not directly related. If listed, 3-1-4 should be somewhere under 3-1 or 3-2 as a tertiary 4M correlation item		3-2-2 Variation in pneumatic pressure	OK
					3-2-3 Wrong lubricant used in pressurizer	OK
					3-2-4 Defective bolt adjustment	OK
					⑧ Not related	
					⑨ 3-2-5 Poor stabilization method	

(Not a secondary correlation for 3-1 (unrelated))

⑥ Should be redesignated as 3-2 (primary item)

7 P-M Analysis Case Studies

THE FIVE EXAMPLES IN THIS CHAPTER are actual narratives of how P-M analysis was used successfully to reduce chronic defects in a manufacturing operation.

CASE 1: CORRECTING OD VARIATION ON A CYLINDRICAL GRINDER (NACHI-FUJIKOSHI)

Among all hydraulic valve components, the spool is especially difficult to manufacture in a way that fully meets precision requirements. Cylindrical grinders are used on the outside of these spools, and the grinding tolerances are very strict. When grinding tapered surfaces, operators were frequently forced to adjust the table angle in compensation. As a result, the automated grinders could not could not be exploited to their fullest potential. Assigning an operator to stand by for these adjustments lowered productivity.

As shown in Figure 7-1, the spool includes two dimensions: A at one end and B at the other. The outer diameter (OD) is automatically measured at A, while B is at the work spindle end. The improvement team attempted to reduce OD variation defects to zero while raising productivity.

FIGURE 7-1: HYDRAULIC VALVE SPOOL

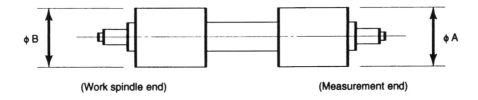

φ B   (Work spindle end)   (Measurement end)   φ A

Clarifying the Defect Phenomena

In the OD measurements for dimensions A and B (Figure 7-2) there is a somewhat greater variation for B. Shop floor operators have remarked that during morning and noon startup, extra care is required for dimensional changes and the table angle must often be adjusted. OD changes reappear during normal operation so they must adjust the table angle or set up dimensional compensation then as well. To understand these conditions better, the team recorded OD measurements for one entire day shift, including morning and noon startup. They allowed no adjustments to the equipment during the course of the survey. Figure 7-3 shows their results.

FIGURE 7-2: SPOOL OD VARIATION

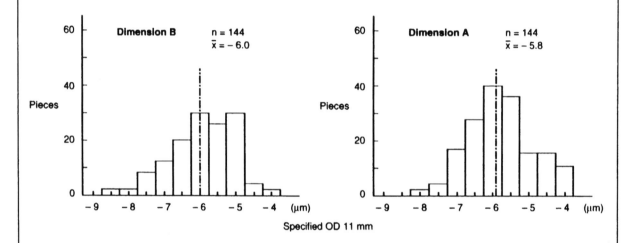

The highest "×" mark represents the measurement end (A), which is controlled by an automatic dimension-setting device. The highest "o" mark represents the work-spindle end (B). Among other things, the survey showed precision at the work-spindle end going from on target (0 microns) at 8:00 AM to -8 microns in just 20 minutes.

The bottom section of Figure 7-3 shows histograms of dimensional variation for both ends between 8:00 AM and 4:00 PM. The survey indicates more overall variation in both A and B than what was reflected in the original data (Figure 7-2).

When the team began this improvement project, they believed they were dealing with a single defect phenomenon. After reviewing the survey results, they realized that, in fact, four distinct phenomena required attention (see Figure 7-4).

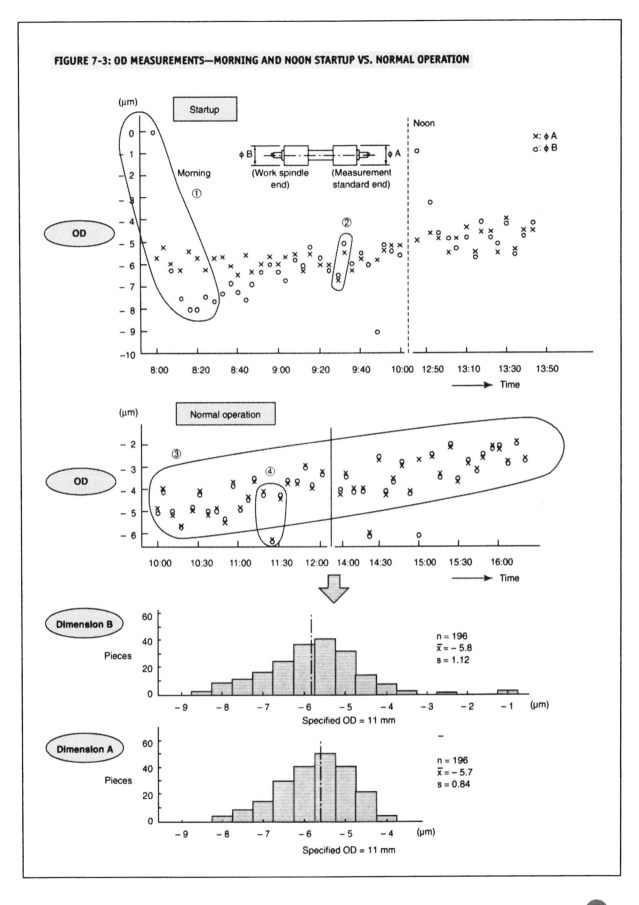

FIGURE 7-3: OD MEASUREMENTS—MORNING AND NOON STARTUP VS. NORMAL OPERATION

FIGURE 7-4: STRATIFICATION OF DEFECT PHENOMENA

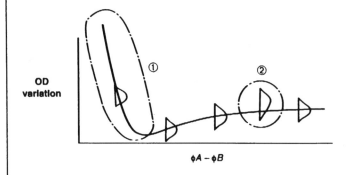

OD
variation

$\phi A - \phi B$

① During startup, the difference between A and B peaked at 5–6 microns, then leveled off to almost zero after about one hour.

② During normal operation, the difference between A and B suddenly increased, then came back down.

③ During normal operation, A tended to run a little higher than B overall.

④ During normal operation, A would suddenly drop below B, then come back up.

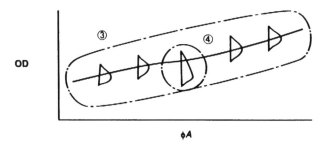

OD

ϕA

Operating Principles and Equipment Mechanisms

The team performed P-M analysis for each phenomenon, but not before studying the operating principles and mechanisms of the equipment (cylindrical grinder) processing these spools.

Figure 7-5 illustrates the operating principles for the cylindrical grinder. The workpiece (spool) is held by a diaphragm chuck. While the workpiece is turned, the grindstone is also turned at high speed. The grinder edge facing the workpiece removes cutting swarf while grinding the workpiece to the specified shape and dimensions. A diamond tool installed on a table automatically adjusts the grinder (0.02 mm two times, 50 pieces/dress).

Figure 7-6 diagrams the hydraulic circuit while Figure 7-7 outlines the grinding cycle.

FIGURE 7-5: CYLINDRICAL GRINDER OPERATING PRINCIPLES AND MECHANISMS

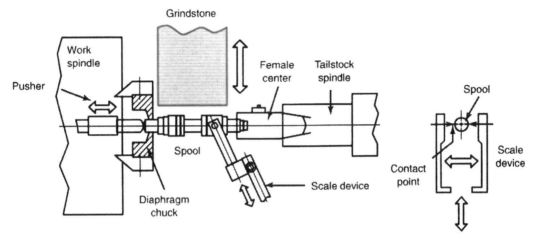

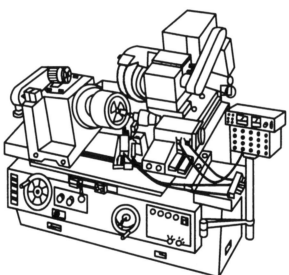

Model GP-35 Cylindrical Grinder
Plunge grinding (with table oscillation)
Direct automatic OD measurement
Diamond tool installed on table automatically adjusts grinder
(0.02 mm two times, 50 pieces/dress)

FIGURE 7-6: HYDRAULIC CIRCUIT DIAGRAM

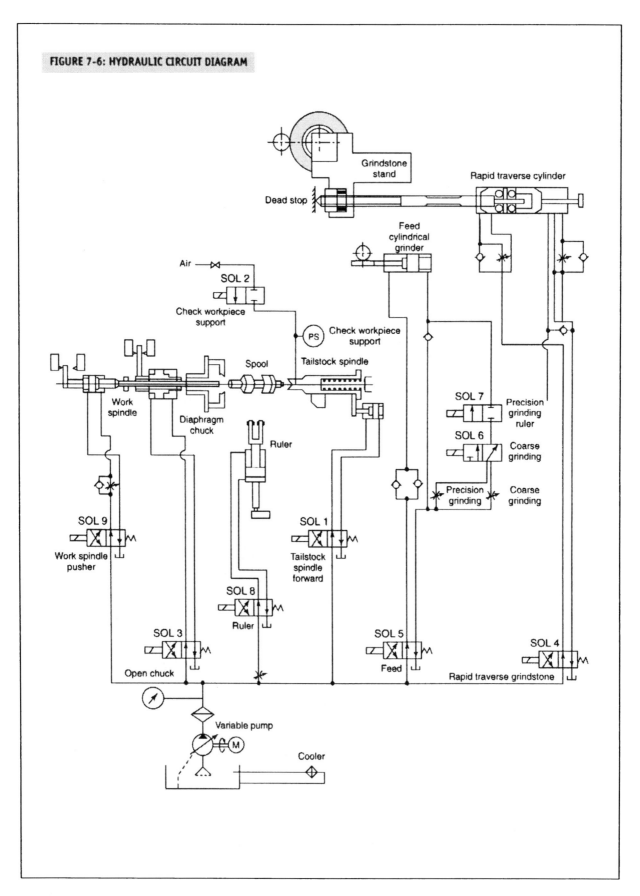

Grinding Cycle

Feed in workpiece ⟶ Set tailstock spindle forward ⟶ Set workpiece against pusher ⟶ Check workpiece support and air ⟶ Close chuck ⟶ Grind (plunge grinding with table oscillation) ⟶ Stop grinding ⟶ Set table stop position ⟶ Open chuck ⟶ Set tailstock spindle back ⟶ Set pusher forward ⟶ Remove workpiece

Cycle Line Chart

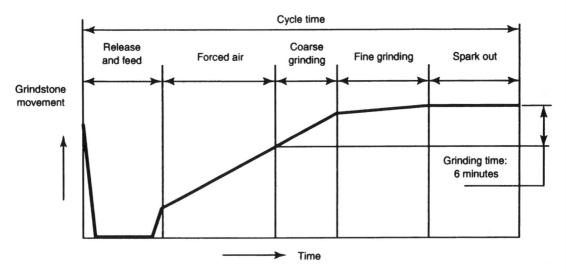

P-M Analysis

After stratifying one defect phenomenon into four and then studying relevant operating principles and mechanisms, the team carried out a P-M analysis for each phenomenon.

Table 7-1 displays the P-M analysis chart for phenomenon 1 and Table 7-2 shows the post-analysis review of survey results. Tables 7-3 through 7-8 reveal the results for the other three phenomena (see pages 122-127).

TABLE 7-1: P-M ANALYSIS TABLE FOR PHENOMENON #1

Part: Wet-type solenoid valve spool

Equipment: Cylindrical grinder

Defect Item: OD variation

Phenomenon	Physical Analysis	Constituent Conditions	Primary 4M Correlations
Large difference between A and B during morning and noon startup periods. $\left(\begin{array}{c}\text{B peaks at 5-6 microns higher than}\\ \text{A, then levels off to slightly smaller}\\ \text{than before startup.}\end{array}\right)$	Workpiece rotational axis was not aligned with grinding surface $\left(\begin{array}{c}\text{Distance between workpiece's}\\ \text{rotational axis changes from } b > a\\ \text{to } b = a\end{array}\right)$	1. Workpiece rotational axis not aligned with grinding surface	1-1 Heat displacement in grindstone spindle
			1-2 Heat displacement in work spindle
			1-3 Heat displacement in tailstock spindle
			1-4 Heat displacement in table
		2. Grinding surface not aligned with grindstone spindle	2-1 Table lateral motion not aligned with grindstone spindle (parallelism during dressing)
			2-2 Grindstone forward and aft motion not perpendicular to grindstone spindle
			2-3 Heat displacement in table

TABLE 7-2: REVIEW OF SURVEY RESULTS FOR PHENOMENON #1

Part: Wet-type solenoid valve spool

Equipment: Cylindrical grinder

Defect Item: OD variation

Check Items	Measurement Methods	Survey Findings			Action	Results
		Standard Values	Measured Values	Evaluation		
Heat displacement in grindstone spindle		Not established	0.025 – 0.042	Action required	1. Do 30 minutes' preparation after startup ① Change cycle time from 78 seconds to 15 seconds ② Run grindstone spindle and work spindle ③ Move grindstone stand and table back and forth ④ Release grinding coolant 2. Dress grindstone right after starting to grind 3. Dress grindstone after every ten workpieces during the 90-minute heat displacement period and then after every 50 workpieces 4. Keep the equipment running during the lunch break	• Beginning with the first workpiece, the difference between A and B was 1 micron or less, with no variation during the startup period • No table angle adjustments were made
Heat displacement in work spindle		Not established	0.01	Action required		
Heat displacement in tailstock spindle		Not established	0	OK	OK	OK
Heat displacement in table		Not established	0.002	OK; difference small enough to be ignored	OK	OK
Parallel alignment of grindstone spindle and table lateral motion		0.01/m	0.007/m	OK	OK	OK
Perpendicular to grindstone stand forward and aft motion		0.01/total length	0.005/total length	OK	OK	OK

TABLE 7-3: P-M ANALYSIS TABLE FOR PHENOMENON #2

Part: Wet-type solenoid valve spool

Equipment: Cylindrical grinder

Defect item: OD variation

Phenomenon	Physical Analysis	Constituent Conditions	Primary 4M Correlations
Occasional differences between A and B during normal operation	Workpiece rotational axis not aligned with grinding surface (changes from $b = a$ to $b \neq a$) 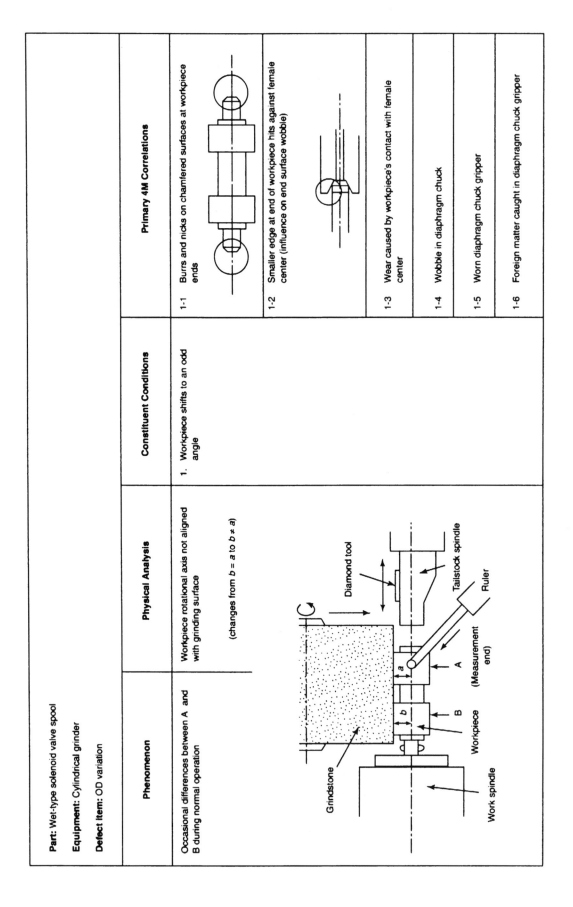	1. Workpiece shifts to an odd angle	1-1 Burrs and nicks on chamfered surfaces at workpiece ends 1-2 Smaller edge at end of workpiece hits against female center (influence on end surface wobble) 1-3 Wear caused by workpiece's contact with female center 1-4 Wobble in diaphragm chuck 1-5 Worn diaphragm chuck gripper 1-6 Foreign matter caught in diaphragm chuck gripper

TABLE 7–4: REVIEW OF SURVEY RESULTS FOR PHENOMENON #2

Part: Wet-type solenoid valve spool

Equipment: Cylindrical grinder

Defect item: OD variation

Check Site	Check Items	Measurement Methods	Survey Findings		Evaluation	Countermeasures	Results
			Standard Values	Measured Values			
Work	Burrs and nicks on workpiece end	Visual	No burrs or nicks allowed	Burrs detected	Action required	1. Revised NC lathe program (previous process) to prevent burrs 2. Added a brush to the top of the grinder chute to remove slight burrs and scale	OK
Work	Taper angle of workpiece end	Industrial microscope	33°	28 to 30 degrees	Action required	Set taper angle to 33° for all workpiece ends so that larger edge OD of workpiece end makes contact with female center	OK
Tailstock	Wear in female center	Dimension gauge	Differential of 0.02	0.03	Action required	Restored (reground)	OK
Tailstock and chuck	Deviation between chuck and center of female center		$\dfrac{0.002}{50}$	0.002	OK	OK	OK
Chuck	Diaphragm chuck wobble		0.005	0.001	OK	OK	OK
Chuck	Chuck gripper wear	Pin gauge	Within φ 6.6	φ 6.45	OK	OK	OK
Chuck	Dirt and debris caught in chuck gripper	Visual	No debris allowed	Dirt and debris detected	Action required	Attached an automatic air blower	OK

TABLE 7-5: P-M ANALYSIS TABLE FOR PHENOMENON #3

Part: Wet-type solenoid valve spool

Equipment: Cylindrical grinder

Defect item: OD variation

Phenomenon	Physical Analysis	Constituent Conditions	Primary 4M Correlations
Variation in A during normal operation (OD variation tends to run about 3 microns positive overall)	Distance a between the workpiece's rotational axis and the grinding surface does not equal half the ruler's measured value d where d is the specified OD value $$\left(\begin{array}{c} \text{Changes from} \\ a = \dfrac{d}{2} \ \text{to} \ a > \dfrac{d}{2} \end{array} \right)$$ 	1. Change in ruler measurement precision	1-1 Precision of measuring head decreases gradually with repeated use
			1-2 Ruler origin point changes (due to temperature drift)
		2. Deviation in ruler measurement position	2-1 Heat displacement in ruler finger (measurement probe)
			2-2 Heat displacement in ruler cross slide
			2-3 Heat displacement in ruler head

TABLE 7-6: REVIEW OF SURVEY RESULTS FOR PHENOMENON #3

Part: Wet-type solenoid valve spool

Equipment: Cylindrical grinder

Defect Item: OD variation

Check Site	Check Items	Measurement Methods	Survey Findings		Evaluation	Action	Results
			Standard Values	**Measured Values**			
	Precision of measurement head after repeated use	Gauge test at constant temperature	n = 25 ± 0.5 μm	n = 25 max + 0.4 μm − 0.3 μm	OK	OK	OK
	Temperature drift	Requested drift test	Not established	1. Amp + measurement head = 2.7 μm (9H) 2. Amp = 2.0 μm (5H)	Action required	Installed new amp that is not affected by temperature changes (includes ambient temperature compensation module)	Temperature drift not detected; OK
	Heat displacement in finger		Not established	Expansion (measured value) $100 \times 10 \times 1.2 \times 10^{-5}$ = 0.012	Impact on diameter = 0.013 microns	OK	OK
Ruler	Heat displacement in cross slide		Not established	0.002	Difference is small enough to be ignored	OK	OK
	Heat displacement in head		Not established	0.001	Difference is small enough to be ignored	OK	OK

TABLE 7-7: P-M ANALYSIS TABLE FOR PHENOMENON #4

Part: Wet-type solenoid valve spool

Equipment: Cylindrical grinder

Defect item: OD variation

Phenomenon	Physical Analysis	Constituent Conditions	Primary 4M Correlations
Variation in A dimension (ruler side) during normal operation period	The distance a between the workpiece rotational axis and the grinding surface does not equal half of the measured value d Changes to $a < \dfrac{d}{2}$ 	1. Deviation in ruler contact point measurement position (variation in position of finger front tip)	1-1 Loose contact point clamp bolt
			1-2 Loose contact point coupling bolt
			1-3 Loose lock nut that sets the position of the ruler front edge
			1-4 Loose cross slide lock nut
		2. Dirt and debris caught between ruler contact point and workpiece	2-1 Worn contact point
			2-2 Particles, grinder swarf, or other debris in grinding coolant
		3. Variation in ruler instructions and timing of grindstone removal	3-1 Shift in position of auto control and adjustment knobs (feed-in occurs when spark-out is finished)

TABLE 7–8: REVIEW OF SURVEY RESULTS FOR PHENOMENON #4

Part: Wet-type solenoid valve spool

Equipment: Cylindrical grinder

Defect Item: OD variation

Check Site	Check Items	Measurement Methods	Survey Findings		Evaluation	Countermeasures	Results
			Standard Values	Measured Values			
Ruler	Variation in finger front tip position	25 repetitions	0.03	n = 25 s = 1.408 μm	Impact on diameter = 0.0003 μm (for 6 pieces)	OK	OK
	Loose contact point clamp bolt	Bolt tightness check	No looseness allowed	No looseness found	OK	OK	OK
	Loose contact point coupling bolt	Bolt tightness check	No looseness allowed	No looseness found	OK	OK	OK
	Loose lock nut on ruler front edge	Bolt tightness check	No looseness allowed	No looseness found	Action required	Tightened bolts	OK
	Loose cross slide lock nut	Bolt tightness check	No looseness allowed	No looseness found	OK	OK	OK
	Worn contact point	Industrial microscope	φ 0.4	Found abrasion measuring 1.2	Action required	Restored (replaced with new part)	OK
Grinding coolant	Contamination	Millipore measurement		20.4 mg of contaminant in 100 cc of coolant	Action required	Changed to a paper filter	8 mg of contaminant in 100 cc of coolant
Grindstone stand	Feed occurs when sparkout is finished	Used visigraph to measure grindstone motor load voltage	0.03 kW	0.03 kW	OK	OK	OK

One of the causes these P-M analyses uncovered was heat displacement. Once grinding started, it took longer to reach thermal equilibrium in the *grindstone spindle* (60 to 90 minutes) than in the work spindle (15 to 20 minutes). This time differential caused the *work spindle* OD (B) to first contract 7 to 8 microns, then expand until it was 1 or 2 microns *over* the pre-grinding dimension. Figure 7-8 shows the relationship between heat displacement over time and OD dimensions at each end of the spool.

FIGURE 7-8: SPINDLE HEAD HEAT DISPLACEMENT AND OD VARIATION

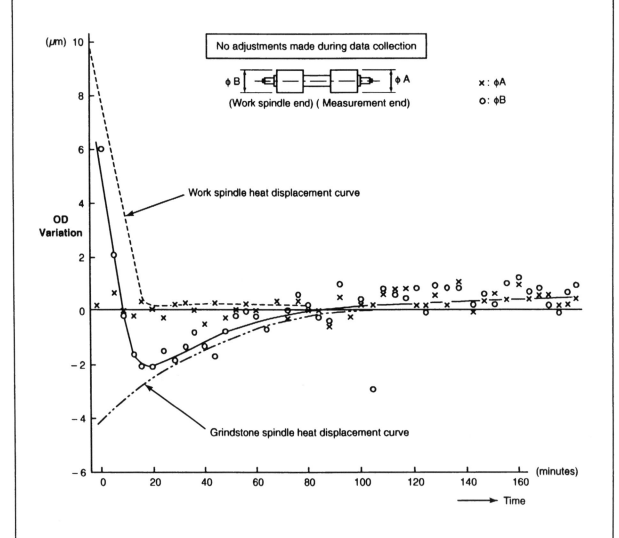

Improvements and Results

The team learned from the equipment manufacturer that its design accounted for heat displacement; the amount they experienced was therefore abnormal. Since a major capital improvement was not cost-justifiable, they took the next best option, a method change. To lessen OD variation due to heat, the team shortened the dressing interval during the first 90 minutes after startup. The interval was cut from once every 50 workpieces to every 10 workpieces, thus compensating for displacement until both spindles reached thermal equilibrium.

These simple actions eliminated the need for table angle adjustments while maintaining OD variation of both ends A and B to within 1 micron. Dimensional defects during startup were reduced to zero.

Figure 7-9 displays the combined effect of improvements for all four defect phenomena. A quick glance at the histogram reveals that OD variation was cut by two-thirds for B and half for A.

As part of this project the team implemented other improvements. They

- installed a calendar timer to run the grinder for 30 minutes prior to the morning shift to prevent defects after startup

- revised the NC lathe program to prevent burrs on the workpiece ends

- attached an automatic air blower to the grinder to keep foreign matter out of the chuck

- reground workpiece ends to better fit into the female center to prevent wear

- attached an ambient temperature compensation module to the ruler to prevent temperature drift

- replaced the ruler diamond tip to prevent wear, and

- changed the grinder coolant filter to a paper filter to reduce contamination of coolant.

Preventive Measures

After confirming the results of the P-M analyses described above, the team developed a qualit-maintenance matrix showing equipment maintenance points and standard values.[1] "Quality maintenance," a methodology developed at Nachi-Fujikoshi, aims to control equipment factors that directly influence quality characteristics.

---

1 *For a complete review of quality maintenance activities, see Nachi-Fujikoshi Corporation, ed.,* Training for TPM *(Productivity Press, 1989), and T. Suzuki, ed.,* TPM in Process Industries *(Productivity Press, 1994).*

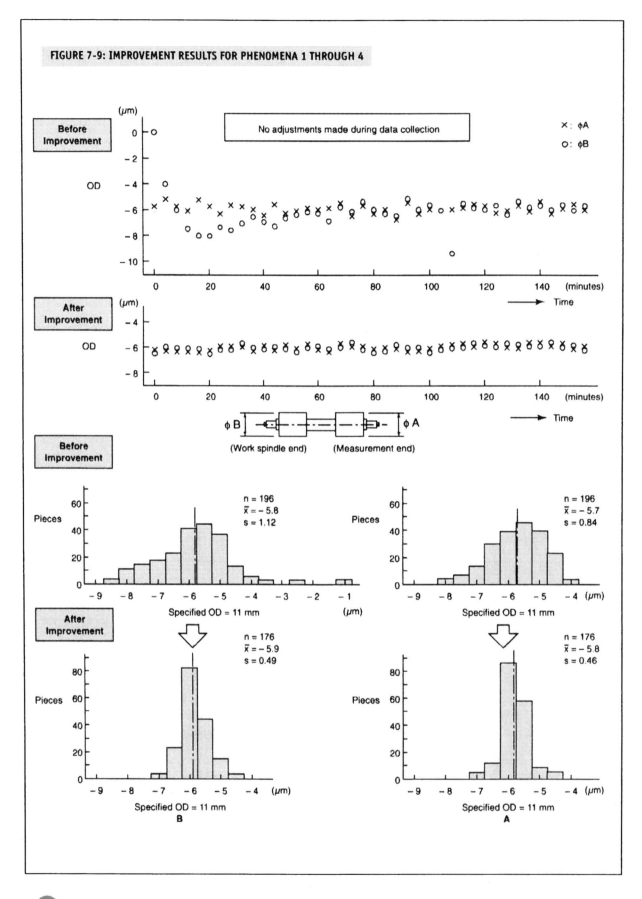

FIGURE 7-9: IMPROVEMENT RESULTS FOR PHENOMENA 1 THROUGH 4

The checklist items in this chart were added to autonomous maintenance and planned maintenance standards and procedures. These new items were standardized as part of this improvement project:

- Added to operator maintenance standards: check for wear in female center, wear in ruler diamond tip, contamination of paper filter

- Added to planned maintenance manual: check for grindstone spindle vibration (monitor trends)

The team also set up SPC charts to monitor and control improvement results over time.

Having come this far through P-M analysis, they continued to work for standardization as part of their quality maintenance program. In addition to OD dimensions, other quality characteristics addressed in this process included cylindricality, roundness, and surface roughness.

Next on the team's agenda was carrying out P-M analyses for these characteristics, making quality maintenance matrices of the resulting new standards, and then adding these new standards and check items to both the autonomous maintenance standards and planned maintenance manual—all as part of their condition control activities to keep the entire process defect-free.

CASE 2: CORRECTING WOBBLE ON THE DISK ROTOR SLIDE OF A TURNING TRANSFER MACHINE (NISSAN)

Nissan uses a turning transfer machine (a type of fully automated lathe) to machine disk brake rotors for automotive wheels (Figure 7-10). Immediately following the machine's installation, the improvement team took measures against process defects that occurred during cutting tool replacement and changeover. One chronic defect in particular—wobble in the rotor disk slide (Figure 7-11)—lowered process capacity to C_p = 0.7 or 0.8.

Although the improvement measures raised process capacity to C_p = 1.2, slide wobble still occurred periodically. When it did, the machine, which had been outfitted with a built-in slide wobble detector, would then switch out of automated operation, thus lowering machine utilization.

This problem prompted the team to apply what they had learned about P-M analysis and effective improvements through an in-house training course. Later, they used those results to further deploy quality maintenance. The project began with the cooperation of manufacturing engineering and maintenance staff.

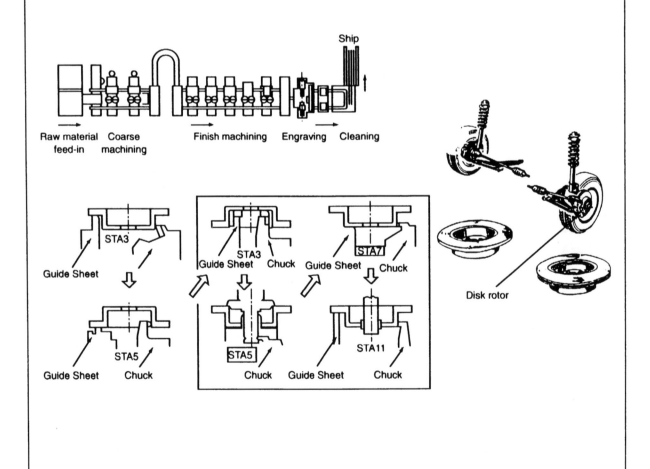

Pareto Chart

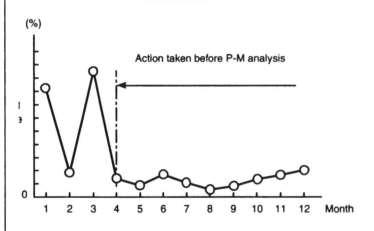

(%)
100
80
60
40
20
0

es

Slide wobble
Hub fitting diameter
Slide thickness
Unfinished slides
Nicks
Other

Slide Machining and Wobble Measurement

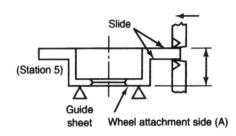

Slide

(Station 5)

Guide sheet

Wheel attachment side (A)

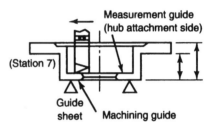

Measurement guide (hub attachment side)

(Station 7)

Guide sheet

Machining guide

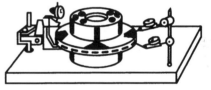

Defect Trends

(%)

Action taken before P-M analysis

0

1 2 3 4 5 6 7 8 9 10 11 12   Month

P-M Analysis

The team's first P-M analysis addressed phenomena that appeared at the final process (Station 7). Subsequent analyses were performed at previous processes on parts whose causal factors stemmed from those processes.

After conducting the physical analysis and identifying constituent conditions, the team worked toward a better understanding of the equipment mechanisms involved. Their main sources were operation manuals and, as much as possible, assembly drawings supplied by manufacturers. Team members also prepared sketches of the mechanisms, such as shown in Figure 7-12.

Next, the team flushed out the primary and secondary 4M correlations for each constituent condition (Table 7-9 on pages 136-137). Since one of these conditions was related to a previous process (Station 5), it was analyzed as a separate phenomenon. Afterward, they reviewed the remaining causal factors with the maintenance staff and modified the list as needed (Table 7-10 on pages 138-140).

FIGURE 7-12: STATION 5 MECHANISMS

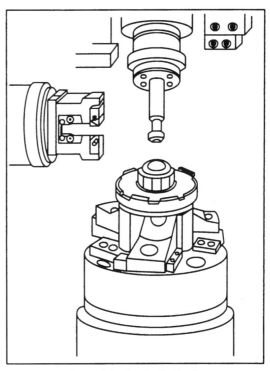

General drawing for Station 5

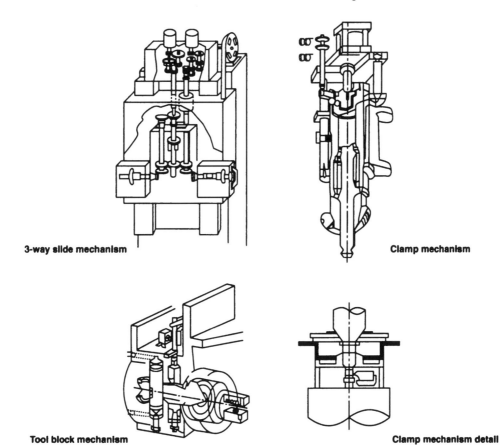

3-way slide mechanism

Clamp mechanism

Tool block mechanism

Clamp mechanism detail

TABLE 7-9 (1): P-M ANALYSIS TABLE

Station 7: No. 1/2

Constituent Conditions	Survey: Standard Values	Quality Impact	Measurement Methods	Measured Values	Evaluation	Primary Factors	Evaluation	Secondary Factors	Evaluation	2nd Survey Results	Restoration/ Improvements
1. Chuck guide sheet is not perpendicular to workpiece rotational axis	Within 0.01	Large	Wobble	0.03	NG	1-1 Wobble in guide sheet relative to spindle center	NG	1-1-1 Sheet block out of alignment	NG	Must replace sheet block	Replaced sheet block
								1-1-2 Worn in sheet block	NG		
								1-1-3 Loose sheet block mount	NG		
								1-1-4 Gap in sheet block mounting hub	NG		
								1-1-5 Nicks or other damage on sheet block	NG		
						1-2 Wobble in chuck/sheet mounting side relative to spindle center		1-2-1 Chuck out of alignment	O		
								1-2-2 Uneven sheet block mounting side	O		
								1-2-3 Loose chuck anchor bolt	O		
								1-2-4 Nicks or other damage on main spindle mounting side	O		
								1-2-5 Each chuck clamped	NG	Must examine main spindle	(bearing preload tightening)
						1-3 Main spindle wobble relative to spindle center	NG	1-3-1 Main spindle ends not perpendicular	O		
								1-3-2 Nicks or other damage on main spindle surface	O	Unable to examine disassemble	
								1-3-3 Worn in main spindle front bearing	△		
								1-3-4 Worn in main spindle rear bearing	△		(bearing preload tightening)
								1-3-5 Insufficient bearing preloading for main spindle	△		
2. Workpiece guide fits poorly with chuck guide sheet	No gaps allowed	Large	Wobble	Comes loose occasionally	NG	2-1 Dirt and debris caught between workpiece and guide sheet	NG	2-1-1 Magnetism in sheet attracts swarf	NG	Action required to prevent swarf accumulation	• Sheet block replaced (smaller area, anti-magnetic)
								2-1-2 Cutting coolant is sprayed at a poor angle	NG		
								2-1-3 Cutting coolant is not sprayed with enough force to rinse away swarf	NG		
								2-1-4 Swarf mixes with coolant and sticks	NG		• Added swarf runoff pipe
								2-1-5 Swarf accumulates on the workpiece guide	NG		• Cleaned coolant tank / • (Improvements at previous process)
								2-1-6 Burrs accumulate on the workpiece guide	O		• (Causal factors from previous process)
						2-2 Workpiece separates from guide sheet during clamping	NG	2-2-1 Chuck jaw is off center	O		
								2-2-2 Chuck jaw outer edge hits something	NG		
								2-2-3 Loose chuck jaw anchor bolt	O	Jaw wear	Replace with super-hard insert jaw
								2-2-4 Worn chuck jaw actuator	O		
								2-2-5 Insufficient chuck clamping strength	△		

Phenomenon: Wobble sometimes occurs in rotor slide (process capacity should be C_p = 1.2) — Changes in parallel alignment of guide sheet, hub mounting surface (machined at this process), and slide (machined at a previous process) relative to the machining guide

Physical Analysis — 4M Correlations

TABLE 7-9 (2): P-M ANALYSIS TABLE

Station 7: No. 2/2   Date:

Constituent conditions	Standard Values	Quality Impact	Measurement Methods	Survey Results — Measured values	Survey Results — Evaluation	Primary Factors	Evaluation	4M Correlations — Secondary Factors	Evaluation	2nd Survey Results	Restoration/Improvements
						2-3 Workpiece separates from guide sheet during machining	Unk.	2-3-1 Too much swarf	△		(Improvements at previous process)
								2-3-2 Insufficient chuck clamping strength	○		
								2-3-3 Worn in chuck jaw tip	NG		(Replace with super-hard insert jaw)
3. Cutting tool tip's line of motion is not aligned with guide sheet 1. Main slide out of alignment 2. Sub slide out of alignment	Within 0.01	Large	Check against primary 4M correlation			3-1 Looseness in tool holder (addressed before P-M analysis)	OK	3-1-1 Loose tip tightening bolt			Restored
								3-1-2 Loose carriage tightening bolt			←
								3-1-3 Wear in carriage mounting side			←
								3-1-4 Intrusion of debris in carriage mounting			←
								3-1-5 Loose tool block tightening bolt			←
								3-1-6 Worn tool block insert section			
						3-2 Variation in motion of cutting stand's slide unit (addressed before P-M analysis)	OK	3-2-1 Loose cutting stand lower stopper			
								3-2-2 Scuffing and wear in cutting stand slide			
								3-2-3 Loose cutting stand slide tightening bolt			
								3-2-4 Wear in cutting stand slide gib			
						3-3 Change in swarf conditions		3-3-1 Variation in swarf from machining	NG		Restored
								3-3-2 Inconsistent cutting speed	○		(P-M analysis conducted at previous process)
4. Distortion (bending) in Distortion	Within 0.02	Large		0.02	OK	4-1 Bent during chuck clamping		4-1-1 Chuck clamping pressure is too strong			
								4-1-2 Insufficient workpiece surface hardness			
						4-2 Bent during cutting operation		4-2-1 Too much swarf			
								4-2-2 Cutting speed is too fast			
								4-2-3 Worn chip edge			
								4-2-4 Cutting coolant does not rinse well enough			
								4-2-5 Insufficient workpiece surface hardness			
5. Slide surface (machined at station 5) not aligned with workpiece guide at this process	Within 0.02			0.04	NG	(P-M analysis done at previous process)					

TABLE 7-10 (1 through 3): P-M ANALYSIS TABLE (MODIFIED)

Station 7: No. 1/3

				Phenomenon		Physical Analysis			
				Wobble sometimes occurs in rotor slide relative to machining guide.		Changes in parallel alignment of machining guide sheet and slide (machined at this process)			

Constituent Conditions	Standard Values	Impact	1st Survey Methods	Survey Results — Measured Values	Survey Results — Evaluation	4M Correlations — Primary Factors	Eval.	4M Correlations — Secondary Factors	Eval.	2nd Survey Results	Restoration/Improvements
1. Chuck guide sheet is not perpendicular to workpiece rotational axis	Within 0.01	Large		0.03	NG	1-1 Guide sheet surface wobbles relative to spindle center	NG	1-1-1 Sheet ring is out of alignment	NG		Sheet surface reground
								1-1-2 Wear in top of sheet ring	O		(Later, installed new guide sheet with different guide position)
								1-1-3 Nicks or other damage in top of sheet ring	O		
								1-1-4 Loose sheet ring anchor bolt	NG	Needs tightening	
								1-1-5 Gap in sheet ring lower mounting side	O		
						1-2 Chuck mounting side wobbles relative to spindle center	NG	1-2-1 Chuck is out of alignment	O		
								1-2-2 Unevenness in sheet ring mounting side	O		
								1-2-3 Loose chuck anchor bolt	O		
								1-2-4 Nicks or other damage in spindle ends	O		
								1-2-5 Clamping force has moved the chuck out of alignment	NG		(bearing preload tightening)
						1-3 Spindle ends wobble relative to spindle center	△	1-3-1 Spindle ends are not perpendicular	O		
								1-3-2 Nicks or other damage in spindle	O		
								1-3-3 Worn spindle front bearing	△		
								1-3-4 Worn spindle rear bearing	△		(bearing preload tightening)
								1-3-5 Loose spindle bearing preload	△		
2. Workpiece guide fits poorly with chuck guide sheet	No gaps allowed	Large		Comes loose occasionally	NG	2-1 Swarf or other debris caught between workpiece and guide sheet	NG	2-1-1 Magnetism in sheet attracts swarf	NG	Action required to prevent swarf accumulation	Sheet block replaced (replaced with improved antimagnetic sheet)
								2-1-2 Cutting coolant is sprayed at a poor angle	NG		Added swarf run-off pipe
								2-1-3 Cutting coolant is not sprayed with enough force to rinse away swarf	NG		
								2-1-4 Swarf get mixed in with cutting coolant and sticks	NG		Cleaned coolant tank
								2-1-5 Swarf accumulates on the workpiece guide	NG		(Improvements at previous process)
								2-1-6 Burrs accumulate on the workpiece guide	O		(Improvements at previous process)

Process 7: No. 2/3

Constituent Conditions	Standard Values	Impact	1st Survey Methods	Survey Results — Measured Value	Survey Results — Evaluation	Primary Factors	Evaluation	Secondary Factors (4M Correlations)	Evaluation	2nd Survey Results	Restoration/Improvements
						2-2 Lowering of tail slider causes clamped workpiece to come loose from guide sheet	NG	2-2-1 Tension plate hits workpiece	△	Damaged	Repaired
								2-2-2 Tension plate equalization is stiff	○		
								2-2-3 Wear on connecting side of tension plate	○		
								2-2-4 Tension plate is out of alignment	○		
								2-2-5 Insufficient slider pressure	○		
								2-2-6 Sheet is being bent by pressure	○		
								2-2-7 Sheet mounting hub is being bent by slider pressure	○		
								2-2-8 Draw bar center is out of position	○		
								2-2-9 Chuck jaw center is out of position	○		
								2-2-10 Worn chuck tip	NG		Replaced chuck jaw
								2-2-11 Loose chuck jaw anchor bolt	NG		Tightened
								2-2-12 Wear in chuck jaw tapered section	NG		Replaced draw bar
						2-3 Guide sheet separates from workpiece during operation	Unk.	2-3-1 Insufficient chuck clamping	○		
								2-3-2 Insufficient chuck pulling force	△		
								2-3-3 Worn chuck jaw	NG		(Replaced chuck jaw)
								2-3-4 Worn chuck actuator	△		
								2-3-5 Wear on connecting side of tension plate			
								2-3-6 Loose chuck jaw anchor bolt			
								2-3-7 Wear in chuck jaw tapered section			
3. Cutting tool tip motion changes relative to the work-piece rotational axis			Study as primary 4M correlation			3-1 Tip holder movement (made improvement for this before P-M analysis)	OK	3-1-1 Loose tip anchor bolt			Restored
								3-1-2 Wear due to missing tip floor plate			←
								3-1-3 Loose carriage tightening bolt			←
								3-1-4 Wear in carriage mounting side			←
								3-1-5 Intrusion of debris in carriage mounting side			(Improvements at previous process)
								3-1-6 Waviness in machining allowance			

TABLE 7-10 (1 through 3): P-M ANALYSIS TABLE (MODIFIED) (CONTINUED)

Process 7: No. 3/3

Constituent Conditions	Standard Values	Impact	1st Survey Methods	Survey Results — Measured Value	Survey Results — Evaluation	Primary Factors	Evaluation	4M Correlations — Secondary Factors	Evaluation	2nd Survey Results	Restoration/Improvements
						3-2 Motion in index tool holder	OK	3-2-1 Loose holder anchor bolt			
								3-2-2 Unevenness in holder mounting side			
								3-2-3 Intrusion of debris in holder side			
								3-2-4 Cracking in holder			
								3-2-5 Waviness of machining allowance			
						3-3 Variation in cross slider's feed motion	OK	3-3-1 Wear in cross slider guide surface			
								3-3-2 Loose slide anchor bolt			
								3-3-3 Worn slide way surface			
								3-3-4 Loose slide way fastening bolt			
								3-3-5 Wear in slide gib			
								3-3-6 Loose slide gib adjustment bolt			
								3-3-7 Variation in slide lubrication pressure			
						3-4 Movement during lowering of vertical slider	OK	3-4-1 Wear in cross slider's guide surface			
								3-4-2 Loose slide anchor bolt			
								3-4-3 Wear in slide way surface			
								3-4-4 Loose slide way anchor bolt			
								3-4-5 Worn slide gib			
								3-4-6 Loose slide gib adjustment bolt			
								3-4-7 Loose lower edge stopper			
4. Distortion (warping) of workpiece	Within 0.02			0.02	OK	4-1 Distortion during chuck clamping	OK	4-1-1 Excessive chuck clamping force			
								4-1-2 Tension plate hits workpiece			
								4-1-3 Tension plate equalization is stiff			
								4-1-4 Sheet is bent by slider pressure			
								4-1-5 Insufficient workpiece hardness			
						4-2 Distortion during cutting		4-2-1 Machining allowance is too great			
								4-2-2 Machining feed rate is too fast			
								4-2-3 Worn cutting tip			
								4-2-4 Cutting coolant does not rinse well enough			
								4-2-5 Insufficient workpiece hardness			

Improvements

The team ultimately identified 38 abnormalities, and carried out restorations or improvements for them all. Some of these countermeasures are described in Figure 7-13.

Station 7:

- *Replaced the chuck jaw with a super-hard insert jaw that has better wear resistance*
- *Made the chuck guide sheet smaller with a shape that does not attract swarf*
- *Corrected chuck guide sheet wobble to stay within the 0.01 mm tolerance*
- *Added coolant spray nozzle and cleaned coolant tank*

Station 5:

- *Replaced and restored worn components in chuck section and repaired slightly nicked or otherwise damaged components*
- *Aligned chuck jaw and draw bar*
- *Made chuck guide sheet smaller with a shape that does not attract swarf*
- *Corrected chuck guide sheet wobble to stay within the 0.01 mm tolerance*
- *Added a coolant spray nozzle*
- *Tightened preload for spindle bearings*

While process capacity increased considerably, slide surface wobble still pushed the limits at times. Theorizing this might occur only when wobble exists in both Stations 5 and 7, the team made one more change—making the guide sheet at Station 5 compatible with the guide position for Station 7, incorporating the guide sheet improvements described above.

Results

After all improvements were in place, slide surface wobble defects were eliminated and process capacity rose to a lower limit of C_p = 2.8. This case is a classic example of how after other approaches bring defects down to the chronic loss level, P-M analysis takes them all the way to zero (Figure 7-14).

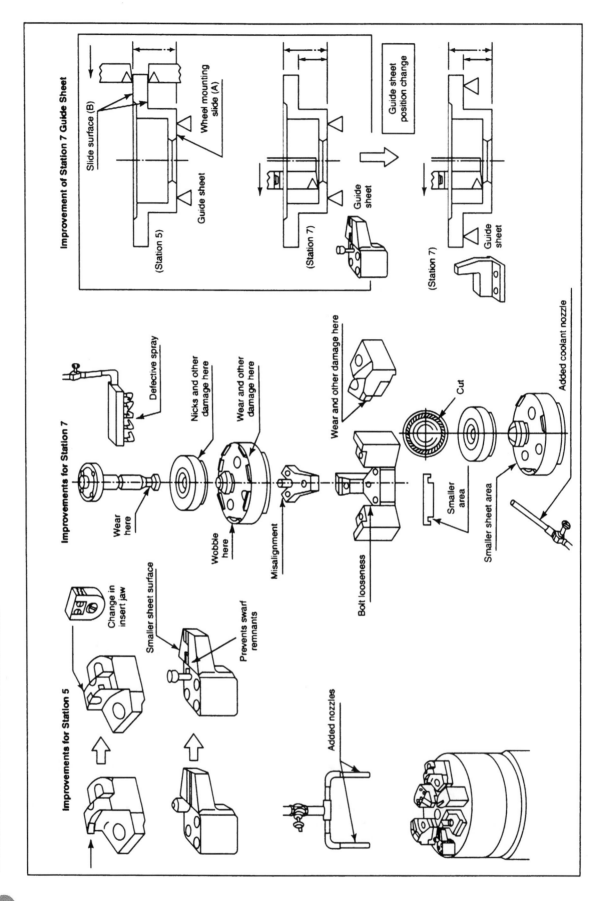

FIGURE 7-13: IMPROVEMENTS FOR STATIONS 5 AND 7

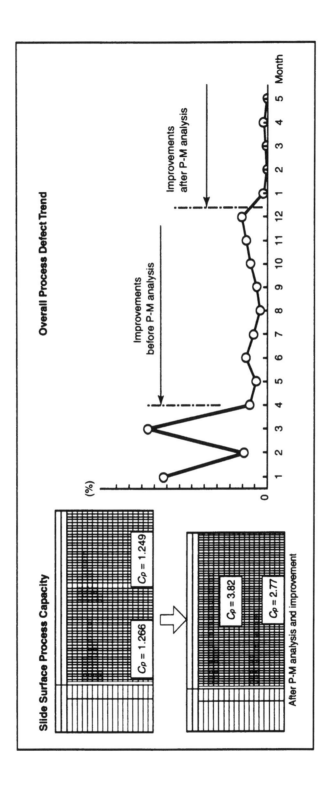

FIGURE 7-14: PROCESS CAPACITY AND DEFECT RATES AFTER IMPROVEMENTS

Overall Process Defect Trend

Improvements after P-M analysis

Improvements before P-M analysis

(%)

Month

Slide Surface Process Capacity

$C_p = 1.266$

$C_p = 1.249$

$C_p = 3.82$

$C_p = 2.77$

After P-M analysis and improvement

Another chronic quality problem addressed through P-M analysis was hub fitting defects. After analysis the hub fitting process capacity rose from $C_p = 0.5$ to a lower limit of 2.6.

Preventive Measures

To help sustain these improvements, the team established optimal (defect-free) conditions based on the quality maintenance philosophy. For each constituent condition verified through P-M analysis, they set up preventive maintenance checks with specified methods, values, and intervals. The values were the same ones used to survey causal factors for abnormalities. This data was organized into a quality maintenance matrix (Figure 7-15). The team also incorporated these new checklist items into the operator maintenance standards to make sure they were carried out.

Future Applications

The team carried out this project as part of the plantwide TPM focused improvement activities. Thanks to a combination of P-M analysis and other activities, they successfully reduced long-standing chronic defects to zero. Having confirmed the effectiveness of this approach, they began applying P-M analysis to eliminate chronic defects in similar processing lines.

FIGURE 7-15 QUALITY MAINTENANCE MATRIX

Part Name: __K10 Rotor__
Part Number: __40206 01B00/21B00/17B00/27B00__

Leader: __Tamura__
Group Leader: _____
Date Revised: _____

Section Head: _____
Engineer: _____
Supervisor: __Takaishi__   __April 3__

Maintenance Check Site Illustrations

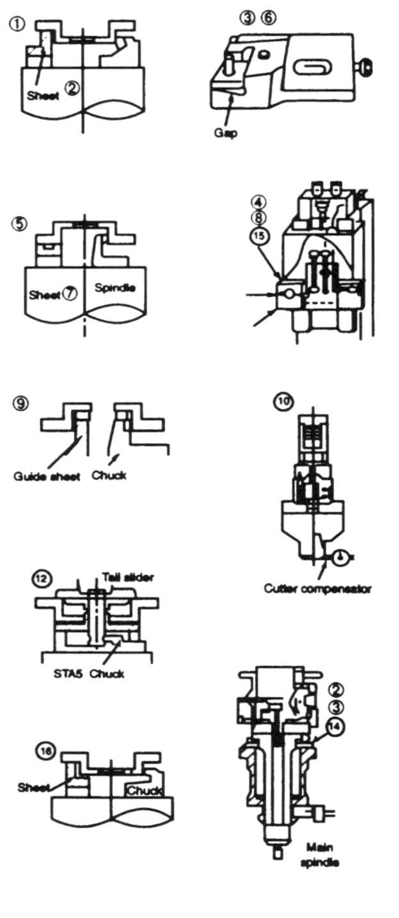

Quality Maintenance Matrix / **Quality Characteristics**

Process	Equipment No.	Maintenance Check Site (equipment, or jig/tool)	Measurement Method	Standard Value	Maintenance Interval	Maintenance Assigned to:	Characteristic Standard Value	Slide surface wobble (Within 0.07)	Slide surface sheet thickness (01B, 21B 12±0.1 / 17B, 27B 15±0.1)	Hub fitting (01B, 17B ø59-0.046 / 21B, 27B ø61 +0.062 +0.016)
1	T-467	STA3 guide sheet wobble	Test indicator	Within 0.01	1/mo.	O.P		O		
2		STA3 main spindle	Machine checker	Low range within P.1.0	←	←			O	
3		STA3 holder cutting tool attachment	Gap gauge	Within 0.01	←	←			O	
4		STA3 slide backlash	Test indicator	Within 0.1	←	←			O	
5		STA5 guide sheet wobble	Test indicator	Within 0.01	←	←		O	O	
6		STA5 holder cutting tool attachment	Gap gauge	Within 0.01	←	←			O	
7		STA5 main spindle	Machine checker	Low range within P.1.0	←	←			O	
8		STA5 slide backlash	Test indicator	Within 0.1	←	←			O	
9	T-468	STA 3 guide sheet wobble	Test indicator	Within 0.01	←	←			O	O
10		STA3 cutter compensator	1/1000 dial gauge	2 microns	←	←			O	O
11		STA5 guide sheet	Test indicator	Within 0.01	←	←		O	O	
12		STA5 tail slider alignment	←	←	←	←			O	
13		STA5 holder cutting tool attachment	Gap gauge	Within 0.01	←	←			O	
14		STA5 main spindle	Machine checker	Low range within P.1.0	←	←			O	
15		STA5 slide backlash	Test indicator	Within 0.01	←	←			O	
16		STA7 guide sheet wobble	←	←	←	←		O		

CASE 3: STABILIZING THE ELECTRON BEAM IN A VACUUM EVAPORATION DEVICE (KANSAI NIPPON DENKI)

Semiconductor metallizing diffusion processes use evaporation devices of the type shown in Figure 7-16 to form an aluminum wiring grid on wafers. In this example, the electron beam used to melt the aluminum was wandering from its prescribed position and melting the copper hearth. This contaminated the interior of the equipment and resulted in significant rework and equipment repair costs (Figure 7-17). The improvement team used P-M analysis to track down the cause of the problem and then took action to stabilize the electron beam.

Clarifying the Defect Phenomena

The position of the electron beam in the device would gradually change and become uncontrollable (Figure 7-18). Improper beam location indicated a shift in the angle of deflection, and this shift became the focus of P-M analysis.

P-M Analysis

Through physical analysis team members were able to link the phenomenon to the X-coil mechanism (Figure 7-19). After working through three levels of causal factors, they identified the cause of X-coil defects as gradual, heat-induced deterioration of the insulation between coil wires. They inferred that current was flowing on both the coil surface and the core, thus diminishing the *effective* current. This led to a weaker magnetic field and a misdirected electron beam, even though *nominal* coil current was constant. The completed P-M analysis table and a review of survey results appear in Tables 7-11 and 7-12.

Improvements

The team decided to improve the cooling system to prevent these heat-induced defects. The X-coils used until this time had relied on natural cooling, which seemed inefficient in terms of equipment design. Based on the melting point of aluminum, estimated coil temperature under existing conditions was between 200° and 300°C. The team modified the equipment so that coolant could be forced into the system, thus lowering the coil temperature to below 100°C.

Results

As shown in Figure 7-20 and Table 7-13, the team achieved its projected results and eliminated the X-coil problems completely.

FIGURE 7-16: VACUUM EVAPORATION DEVICE

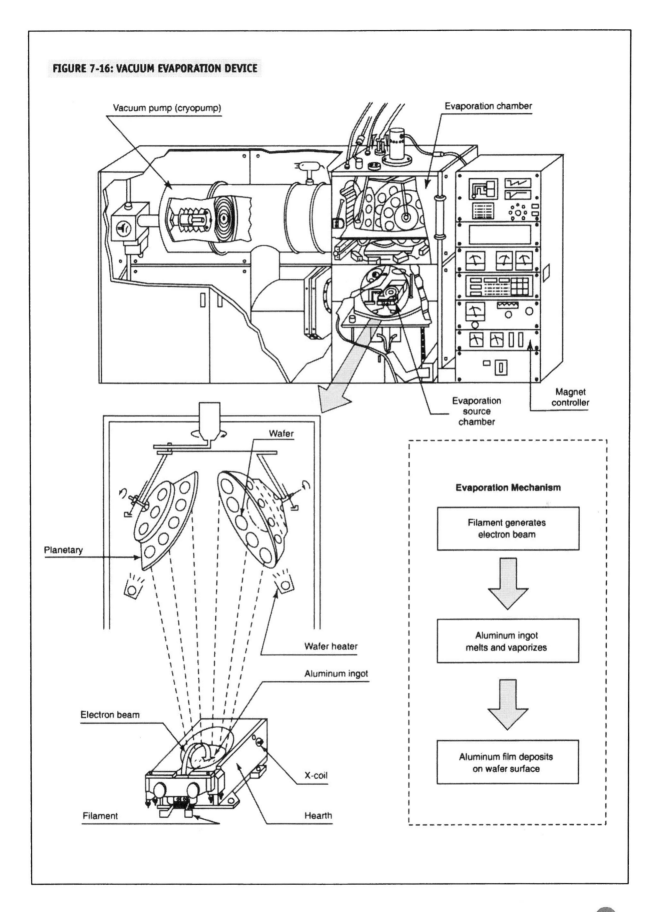

Vacuum pump (cryopump)

Evaporation chamber

Evaporation source chamber

Magnet controller

Wafer

Planetary

Wafer heater

Aluminum ingot

Electron beam

X-coil

Filament

Hearth

Evaporation Mechanism

Filament generates electron beam

Aluminum ingot melts and vaporizes

Aluminum film deposits on wafer surface

FIGURE 7-17: LOSSES DUE TO IMPROPER BEAM POSITION

Mislocated Electron Beam

⇩

1. Contamination of equipment interior
2. Equipment repair cost (maintenance labor)
3. Product rework costs (production labor)
4. Repair part costs (maintenance materials)

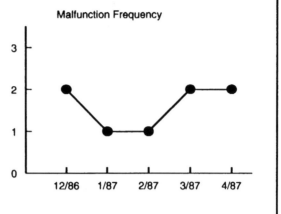

Malfunction Frequency

FIGURE 7-18: ELECTRON BEAM PATH

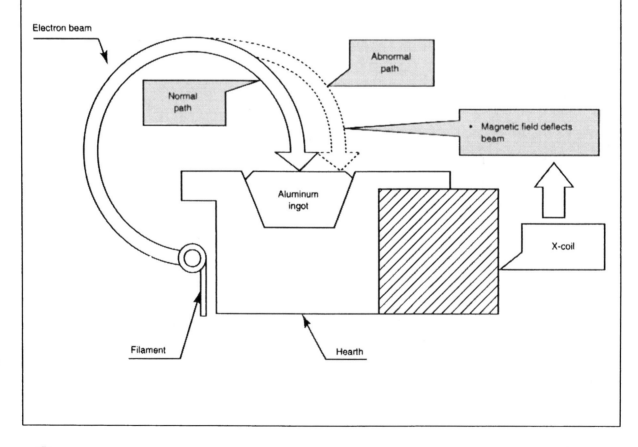

FIGURE 7-19: X-COIL MAGNETISM AND BEAM POSITION

X-coil Functions

Current passes
through X-coil

⬇

Magnetic field is
created

⬇

Electron beam shifts in proportion
to the magnetic field (following
Fleming's left hand rule)

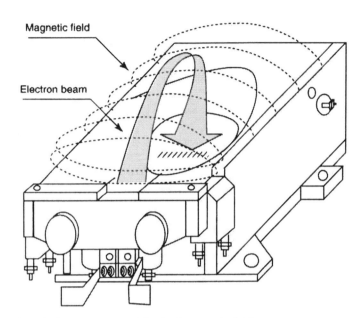

Magnetic field

Electron beam

(Model of electron beam deflection in magnetic field)

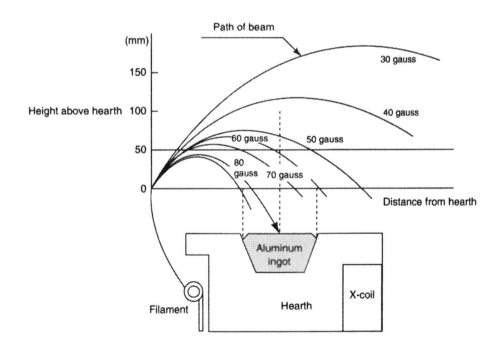

TABLE 7-11: P-M ANALYSIS TABLE

Electron Beam Displacement in Evaporation Device

Phenomenon	Physical Analysis	Constituent Conditions		Primary 4M Correlations		Secondary 4M Correlations	
		Items (diagram)	Allowable range	Items (diagram)	Allowable range	Items (diagram)	Allowable range
Electron beam gradually wanders from center of aluminum ingot	Electron beam deflection angle changes	1. Decreasing beam acceleration voltage	10 KVDC ± 2%	1-1 High tension power source irregularities	10 KVDC ± 2%	1-1-1 Lowered output voltage (100 VAC)	± 5%
						1-1-2 Lowered output voltage (10 KVDC)	± 2%
						1-1-3 Damaged or deteriorated power source components	—
				1-2 Faulty insulation of acceleration voltage (high tension lead terminals)	1000 MΩ or above	1-2-1 Improperly mounted high tension lead terminals	—
						1-2-2 Metallic film on lead terminal insulation	—
						1-2-3 Dirt in high tension lead terminals	—
				1-3 Faulty insulation of beam generator components	1000 MΩ or above	1-3-1 Filament distortion	0.5 ± 0.2 mm
						1-3-2 Small gap between beam former and filament	
						1-3-3 Loose screws	
Electron beam consistently deflects toward the X-coil		2. Weakening beam deflection voltage	80 gauss ± 2%	2-1 Defective assembly of parts near hearth	No gaps anywhere	2-1-1 Gap between hearth and hearth deck	no gaps anywhere
						2-1-2 Hearth deck distortion	
						2-1-3 Loose X-coil mounting screws	
				2-2 Decreased current in X-coil	2.8A ±1%	2-2-1 Lowered input voltage at magnet controller	200 VAC ± 5%
						2-2-2 Lowered output voltage at magnet controller	10 VDC MAX
				2-3 Shortening of effective X-coil wire length	—	2-3-1 Deteriorated insulation between coil wires	500 KΩ or above
				2-4 Equivalent parallel resistance with X-coil	—	2-4-1 Improper insulation of X-coil terminals	500 KΩ or above
						2-4-2 Improper insulation between X-coil wires and core	500 KΩ or above
						2-4-3 Poor coating of coil wires	—
						2-4-4 Poor insulation of wire lead terminals	500 KΩ or above

TABLE 7-12: REVIEW OF SURVEY RESULTS

Part	Check Items (to control conditions)	Condition Settings — Standard Values	Condition Settings — Quality Impact	Measurement Method (diagram)	Survey Results — Measured Values	Survey Results — Quality Impact	Evaluation	Improvements	Results
High tension power source	Input voltage	200 VAC ±5%	—	Tester	201 VAC	No effect	OK	OK	OK
	Output voltage	10 KVDC ±2%	Thinner evaporation deposit	High tension voltmeter	10 KVDC	No effect	OK	OK	OK
	Damage to components	No burns or damage	—	Sight; measure resistance with tester	No irregularities	—	OK	OK	OK
High tension lead terminals	Terminal-to-ground insulation	1000 MΩ or above	High tension power source overload		500M	No effect	Improvement required	1. Clean lead terminals 2. Attach terminal covers	1000 MΩ or above
	Coil terminal insulation	500 KΩ or above	Thinner evaporation deposit		20 KΩ	No particular impact other than long evaporation times	Improvement required	1. Clean terminal components 2. Attach terminal covers	1 MΩ
	Resistance in coil wires	2.9 Ω ±5% (2.76 to 3.05)	Irregular evaporation deposit		1.6 – 1.9 Ω	No effect on quality, but electron beam cannot be controlled	Improvement required		OK
X-coil	Heat resistance of coil wire insulation	—	—	—	Teflon/260°C	—	Improvement required	Rebuild to allow forced water cooling of coil interior	Good
	Temperature near hearth during evaporation	—	—	Inferred from melting point of aluminum	200 ~ 300° C	—	Improvement required		→
	Cooling system for hearth vicinity (evaporation parameters)	—	—	Visual inspection and review of drawings	Water cooling only for hearth deck and hearth; X-coil cooled by natural radiation		Improvement required		No changes in beam position since 6/87

FIGURE 7-20: FREQUENCY OF X-COIL MALFUNCTIONS

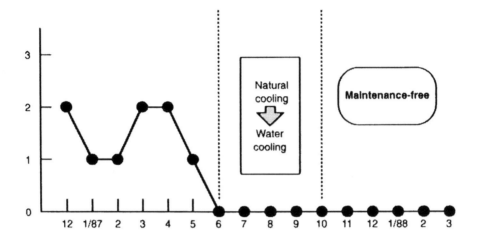

TABLE 7-13: IMPROVEMENT RESULTS

Cost Item	Before Improvement	After Improvement
1. Repair parts (maintenance materials)	3,600	0
2. Equipment repair (maintenance labor)	860	0
3. Product rework (production labor)	1,260	0
Total cost	5,720	0

Preventive Measures

Coil resistance and current data from the P-M analysis survey enabled the team to set "alarm limits" in order to predict deterioration of the X-coil when the beam was correctly located (Figure 7-21). Preventive maintenance based on these values is still underway, but no X-coil deterioration has been observed since the improvements were made (Figure 7-22).

FIGURE 7-21: COIL RESISTANCE AND CURRENT

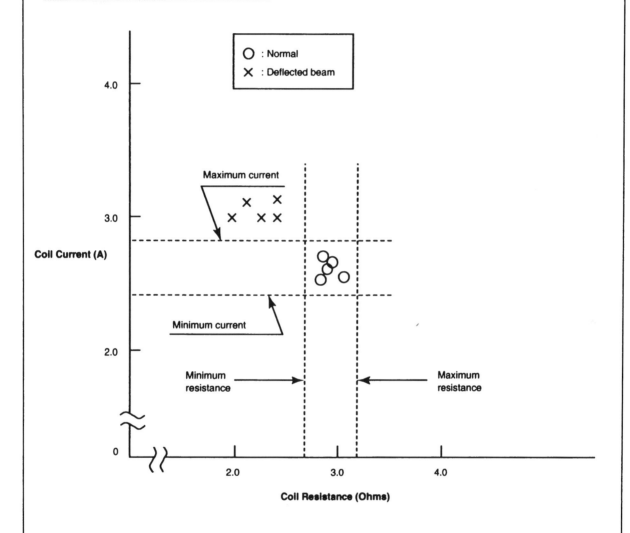

FIGURE 7-22: COIL RESISTANCE AND CURRENT AFTER IMPROVEMENTS

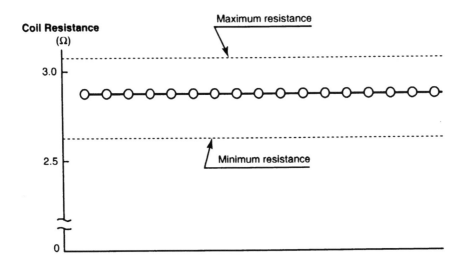

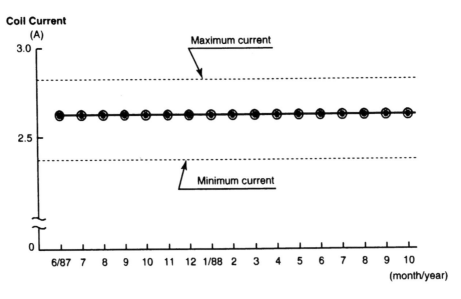

CASE 4: CORRECTING PRINTING SIDE ESTIMATION ERRORS ON A ROTARY PRINTING PUNCH (DAI NIPPON INSATSU)

Rotary printing punches are machines that print and punch box-shaped impressions onto rolled paper. In its printing mechanism, the plate cylinder moves rapidly to the left or right during printing, and the process was experiencing chronic loss due to printing side estimation errors. Since these errors accounted for almost 20 percent of all minor stoppages (Figure 7-23), they became the target of an improvement project.

Since this phenomenon occurred regardless of product or paper type, the improvement team surmised that the problem was mechanical. They replaced those components that seemed the most likely suspects, but to no avail. In fact, after the replacements in printing side estimation, errors shot up to 18 in one month.

That was when the team decided to try P-M analysis.

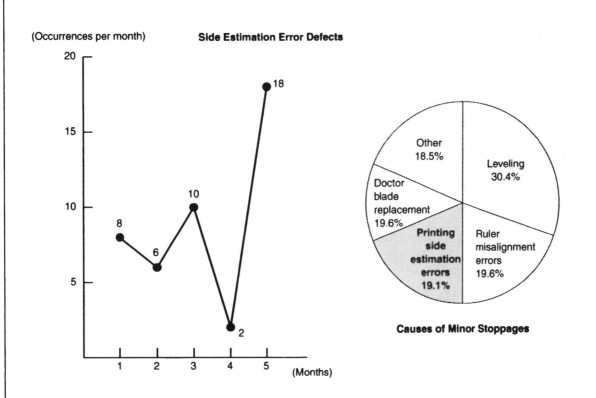

P-M Analysis and Improvements

Team members began by studying the principles behind printing side estimation errors, and did a physical analysis to better understand the phenomenon. They disassembled the plate cylinder (the coupling and coupling bearings), and made sketches of its components during a P-M analysis.

Table 7-14 shows the P-M analysis results and Figure 7-24 highlights the abnormalities the team identified. In this case, the coupling and coupling bearing are the mechanisms analyzed for constituent conditions, and there is only a primary level of 4M correlations.

FIGURE 7-24: ABNORMALITIES IDENTIFIED THROUGH P-M ANALYSIS

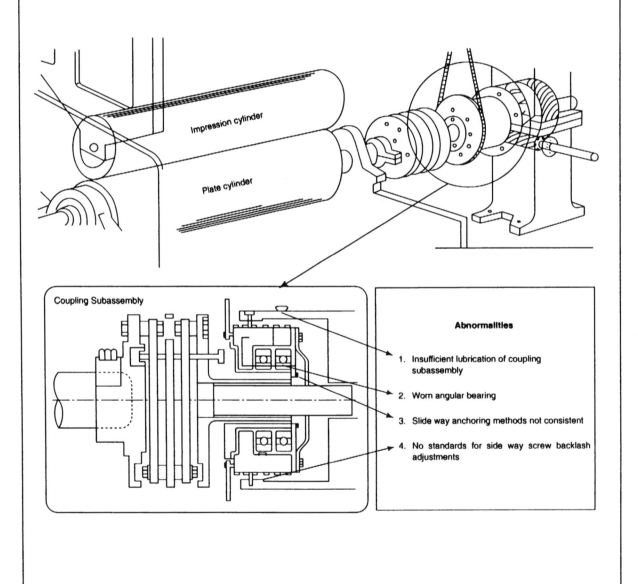

Impression cylinder

Plate cylinder

Coupling Subassembly

Abnormalities

1. Insufficient lubrication of coupling subassembly

2. Worn angular bearing

3. Slide way anchoring methods not consistent

4. No standards for side way screw backlash adjustments

TABLE 7-14: P-M ANALYSIS OF PRINTING SIDE ESTIMATION ERRORS

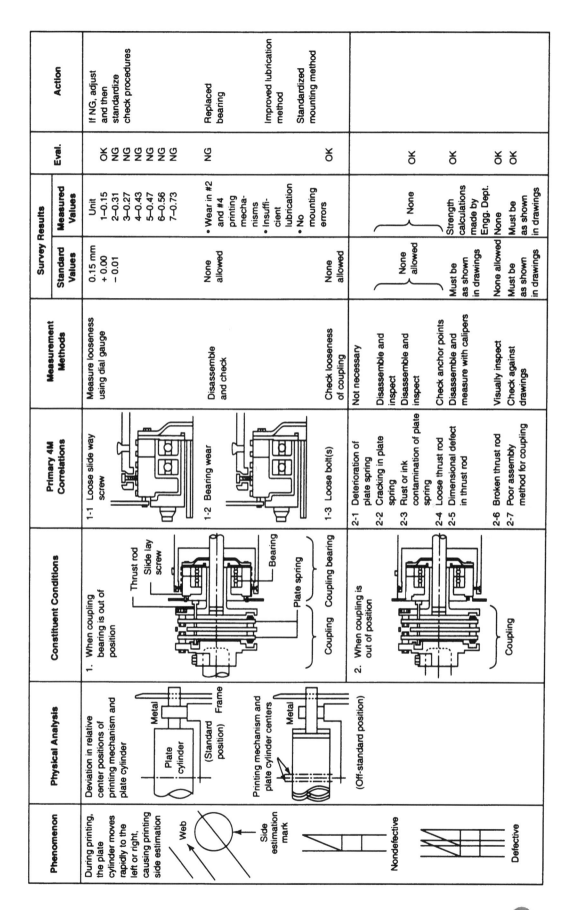

Phenomenon	Physical Analysis	Constituent Conditions	Primary 4M Correlations	Measurement Methods	Survey Results — Standard Values	Survey Results — Measured Values	Eval.	Action
During printing, the plate cylinder moves rapidly to the left or right, causing printing side estimation Web / Side estimation mark Nondefective / Defective	Deviation in relative center positions of printing mechanism and plate cylinder Metal — Frame — Plate cylinder (Standard position) Printing mechanism and plate cylinder centers Metal (Off-standard position)	1. When coupling bearing is out of position Thrust rod / Slide lay screw / Bearing / Plate spring / Coupling / Coupling bearing	1-1 Loose slide way screw	Measure looseness using dial gauge	0.15 mm + 0.00 − 0.01	Unit 1–0.15 2–0.31 3–0.27 4–0.43 5–0.47 6–0.56 7–0.73	OK NG NG NG NG NG	If NG, adjust and then standardize check procedures
			1-2 Bearing wear	Disassemble and check	None allowed	• Wear in #2 and #4 printing mechanisms • Insufficient lubrication • No mounting errors	NG	Replaced bearing Improved lubrication method Standardized mounting method
			1-3 Loose bolt(s)	Check looseness of coupling	None allowed		OK	
		2. When coupling is out of position Coupling	2-1 Deterioration of plate spring	Not necessary	None allowed	None		
			2-2 Cracking in plate spring	Disassemble and inspect				
			2-3 Rust or ink contamination of plate spring	Disassemble and inspect				
			2-4 Loose thrust rod	Check anchor points	Must be as shown in drawings	Strength calculations made by Engg. Dept.	OK	
			2-5 Dimensional defect in thrust rod	Disassemble and measure with calipers		None	OK	
			2-6 Broken thrust rod	Visually inspect	None allowed		OK	
			2-7 Poor assembly method for coupling	Check against drawings	Must be as shown in drawings	Must be as shown in drawings	OK	

These are some of the abnormalities the team uncovered, along with actions they took to correct them:

- **_Insufficient lubrication of coupling._** The lubrication point for the angular bearing is one of a group of centrally located oil inlets. When team members found that the coupling was underlubricated, they installed a separate inlet and increased the lubrication amount and frequency.

- **_Wear in angular bearing._** Inspection of the printing mechanisms revealed worn bearings in #2 and #4, so the team replaced them both.

- **_Inconsistent slide way anchoring methods._** Disassembly and inspection revealed that no two people used the same method of anchoring the slide way. The team standardized the anchoring method and then prepared and conducted a "one-point lesson" to share the new method with all team members.

- **_No standards for slide way screw backlash adjustments._** The slide way screw had too much backlash so the team standardized a method for adjusting it.

Results

As shown in Figure 7-25, these improvements effectively reduced printing side estimation errors from their surge level of 18 per month down to zero. Since about 300 meters of paper roll were lost per stoppage, P-M analysis resulted in a significant material savings.

FIGURE 7-25: IMPROVEMENT RESULTS

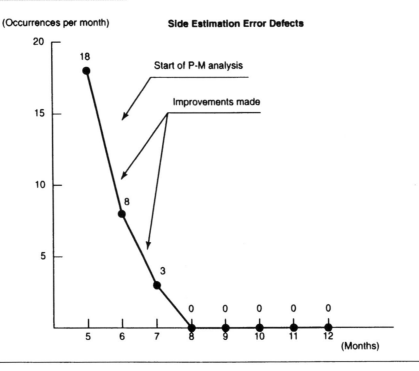

Preventive Measures

The improvement team instituted a preventive maintenance checklist with standard values for all components at risk of deterioration.

Future Applications

For years the team suspected these errors were tied to the plate spring in part of the coupling. When attempts to solve the problem by replacing worn components or substituting a plate spring made of better material did not lead to fruitful results, the team was at a loss. This is what prompted them to apply P-M analysis in earnest.

The team sketched all the mechanisms and components that were being analyzed, which helped members understand their functions and structure more clearly. During this process, they stumbled upon abnormalities in unsuspected places.

For the future, the team plans to avoid the vague reasoning that characterized problem-solving efforts in the past. Instead, they will promote more effective improvement activities which encourage all employees to think in terms of physical principles underlying phenomena.

CASE 5: ELIMINATING OFFSET DEFECTS IN AIR CONDITIONER COMPRESSOR CRANK PINS (DAIKIN)

An examination of the plant breakdown records revealed the single greatest cause of downtime (for quality adjustments)—and the greatest drag on productivity—was the crank machining process for the air compressors (Figure 7-26). These compressors constitute the heart of Daikin air conditioners.

Within this critical process, Pareto analysis first pinpointed the crank pin grinding operation, followed by offset defects from that operation (Figure 7-27). The improvement team recognized a tremendous time and expense would be required to eliminate these chronic quality defects. A variety of analyses and improvements had thus far failed to bring the offset defect rate below a certain level (Figure 7-28). The team decided to try P-M analysis in one more attempt to reach zero defects and eliminate the need for further quality adjustments.

FIGURE 7-26: COMPRESSOR STRUCTURE AND CRANK MACHINING PROCESS

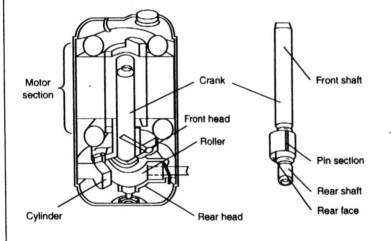

Motor section
Crank
Front head
Roller
Cylinder
Rear head

Front shaft
Pin section
Rear shaft
Rear face

Crank Machining Process
1. Grind front and rear shafts
2. Grind pin section
3. Grind rear face
4. Surface machining
5. Inspection

FIGURE 7-27: PARETO ANALYSIS OF COMPRESSOR QUALITY ADJUSTMENTS

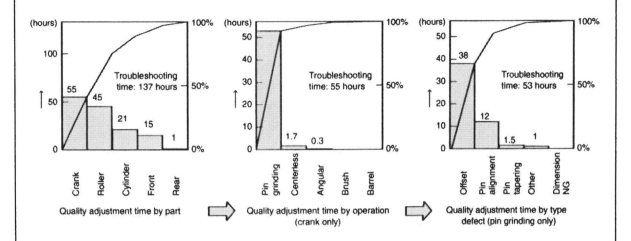

Quality adjustment time by part

Quality adjustment time by operation (crank only)

Quality adjustment time by type defect (pin grinding only)

FIGURE 7-28: OFFSET DEFECT TRENDS

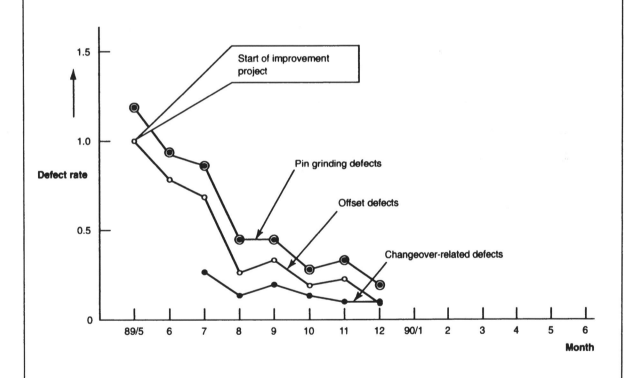

Clarifying the Defect Phenomenon

To acquire a good grasp of the phenomenon, the team conducted 100 percent inspection for a full day, looking for offset defects (Figure 7-29).

The width tolerance is within 18 microns. The more experienced operators were able to get precision within 6 microns through a series of bolt adjustments, such as on the anchor bolts for the chuck body and the retainer. They also had to make a series of adjustments after each changeover, a time when defects are likely to occur.

Operating Principles and Equipment Mechanisms

Figure 7-30 shows the structure of the grinder used on crank pin outer diameters. Figures 7-31 and 7-32 illustrate its main spindle and chuck mechanisms, respectively. Following are the operating principles and standards for crank pin grinding.

Principles

First, the operator fastens an offset jig onto the rotating main spindle. Using the jig, he or she inserts the chuck at an offset distance relative to the main spindle center of rotation. This amount is equal to the offset distance for the workpiece (crank pin).

After chucking the workpiece front shaft, the operator aligns its center of rotation with the main spindle center, then starts rotating the workpiece.

Next, the operator turns the grindstone and lowers it to grind away several cutting burrs that protrude from the workpiece surface, and continues this until the burrs are gone and the workpiece has acquired its finish dimensions.

Standards
- The spindle must be free of wobble
- The main spindle and front shaft centers of rotation must be aligned
- There must not be any change in the distance between the chuck and either center of rotation

FIGURE 7-29: CRANK OFFSET MEASUREMENTS

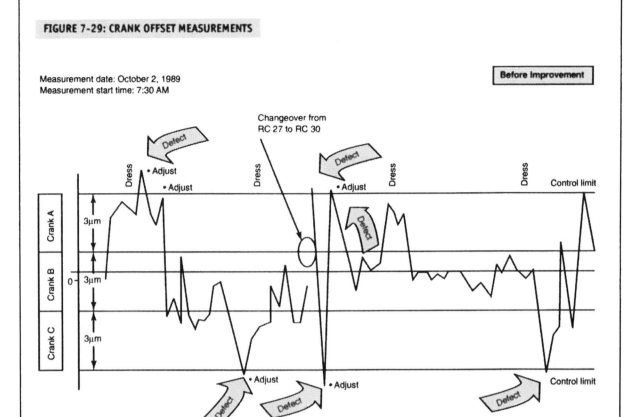

Measurement date: October 2, 1989
Measurement start time: 7:30 AM

Before Improvement

FIGURE 7-30: STRUCTURE OF PIN OD GRINDER

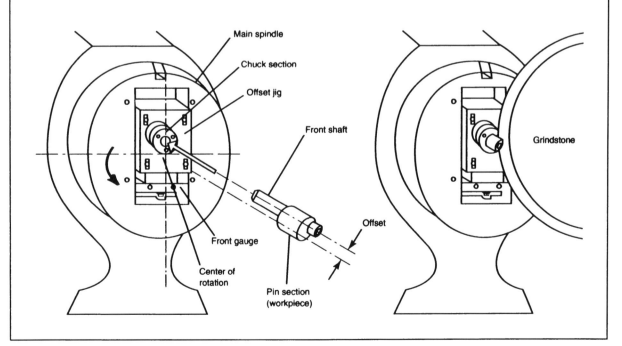

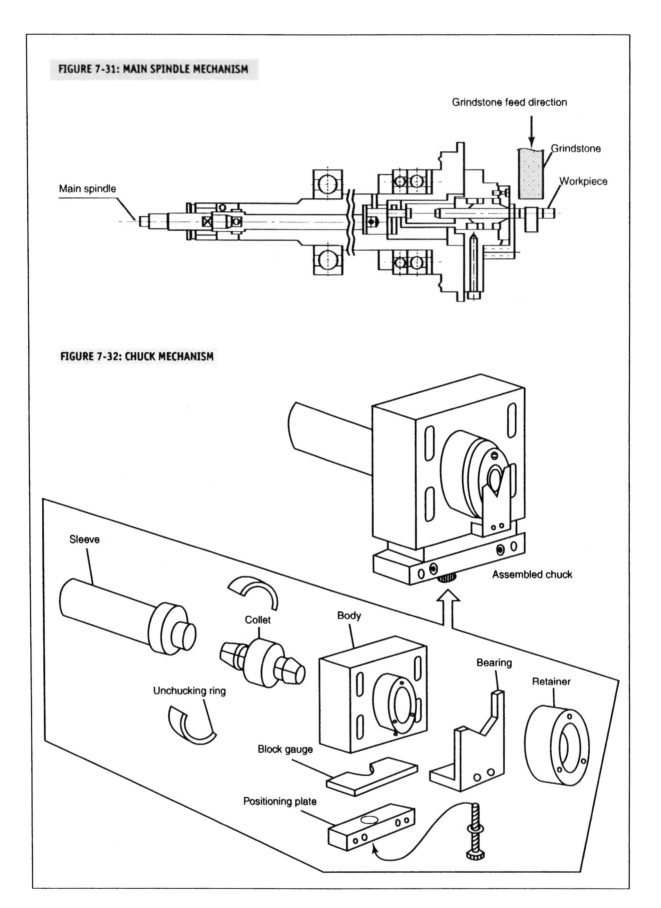

FIGURE 7-31: MAIN SPINDLE MECHANISM

Grindstone feed direction

Grindstone

Workpiece

Main spindle

FIGURE 7-32: CHUCK MECHANISM

Assembled chuck

Sleeve

Collet

Body

Bearing

Retainer

Unchucking ring

Block gauge

Positioning plate

P-M Analysis and Improvements

Tables 7-15 (P-M analysis table, pp. 166-169) and 7-16 (review of survey results, pp. 170-172) reveal what the team discovered about the causes of offset defects and the actions taken to eliminate them.

After surveying all the causal factors identified by P-M analysis, team members restored or improved the conditions associated with each abnormality. Table 7-17 (p. 173) describes some of these countermeasures. In addition, Table 7-18 (p. 174) displays new changeover instructions, which enable even temporary employees to perform changeovers quickly and accurately.

TABLE 7-15 (1 THROUGH 4): P-M ANALYSIS TABLE

Prepared by: Rotary Drive Dept. Machinery Section

Date:

Line: RC small crank
Process: Pin grinding
Equipment: Pin OD grinder
Equipment No.: 79B 3160

Models: RC11 to RC30, RC2 X 17, RC2 X 26
Item: Crank
Drawing No.: 3 PD0436
MQ No.: MCR-018

Quality characteristic: Offset amount
Current condition: 0.2% (defect rate)

Phenomenon: Change in offset during pin grinding (Roundness and parallelism are within standard values)

Physical Analysis	Constituent Conditions			Primary 4M Correlations			Secondary 4M Correlations		
	Items (must be illustrated)	Standard values	Evaluation	Items (must be illustrated)	Standard values	Evaluation	Items (must be illustrated)	Standard values	Evaluation
Change in offset — Change in the distance between the main spindle rotational axis and the marks for the front shaft rotational axis	1. Front shaft rotational axis shifts out of alignment (Illustration shows only one example, this one having a positive shift)			1-1 Chuck body moves		×	1-1-1 Chuck body fastening torque is insufficient (anchor bolts: M8 × 4)	Fastening torque: 120kg/cm	×
							1-1-2 Change in gap between chuck body and spacer		
	2. Front shaft rotational axis tilts			2-1 Large deviation between the front shaft center and the pusher center during chucking		×	2-1-1 Position adjustment error after pusher changeover	Right-left 0.1 – 0.5 mm / Up-down 0.1 – 0.5mm / Loose bolt(s)	× ○ ○

Physical Analysis	Constituent Conditions			Primary 4M Correlations			Secondary 4M Correlations		
	Items (must be illustrated)	Standard Values	Evaluation	Items (must be illustrated)	Standard Values	Evaluation	Items (must be illustrated)	Standard Values	Evaluation
							2-1-2 Pusher moves at an angle	0 – 0.1 mm	O
				2-2 Large deviation between the front shaft center and the workpiece holder's center during chucking			2-2-1 Parallelism adjustment Right-left	0.1 – 0.5 mm	X
							Up-down	0.1 – 0.5 mm	O
							Bolt looseness		O
				2-3 Three collet grips are not evenly fastened during chucking			2-3-1 Edge wear in tapered section of collet retainer	5μ	X
							2-3-2 Edge wear in tapered section of collet	5μ / 9μ	X / O
							2-3-3 Edge wear in tapered section of thrust sleeve	9μ	O

TABLE 7-15 : P-M ANALYSIS TABLE (CONTINUED)

Phenomenon: Change in offset during pin grinding (Roundness and parallelism are within standard values)

Physical Analysis	Constituent Conditions			Primary 4M Correlations			Secondary 4M Correlations		
	Items (must be illustrated)	Standard Values	Evaluation	Items (must be illustrated)	Standard Values	Evaluation	Items (must be illustrated)	Standard Values	Evaluation
				2-4 Deviation in front shaft center after chucking			2-4-1 Backlash in chuck body and thrust sleeve	13 – 18 µm	X
							2-4-2 Not perpendicular to inner diameter of chuck body	5µm	O
							2-4-3 Is the gap between the thrust sleeve and the main spindle gray section correct?	No side contact or pinch-ing allowed	O
				2-5 Workpiece inserted at an angle			2-5-1 Moved toward rear face		X

Phenomenon: Change in offset during pin grinding (Roundness and parallelism are within standard values)

Physical Analysis	Constituent Conditions			Primary 4M Correlations			Secondary 4M Correlations		
	Items (must be illustrated)	Standard Values	Evaluation	Items (must be illustrated)	Standard Values	Evaluation	Items (must be illustrated)	Standard Values	Evaluation
	3 Change in main spindle rotational axis			3-1 Backlash in bearing			Front Section Up-down backlash	≤ 2μ	○
							Right-left backlash	≤ 2μ	○
							Rear section Up-down backlash	≤ 2μ	○
							Right-left backlash	≤ 2μ	○
				3-2 Debris caught in bearing			3-2-1 Not enough forced air on main spindle	Forced air must flow freely	○
				3-3 Loose belt	Not allowed	○			

TABLE 7-16 (1 THROUGH 3): REVIEW OF SURVEY RESULTS

Line: RC small crank
Process: Pin grinding
Equipment: Pin OD grinder
Equipment No.: 79B 3160

Models: RC11 to RC30, RC2 X 17, RC2 X 26
Item: Crank
Drawing No.: 3 PD0436
MQ No.: MCR-018

Quality characteristic:
Offset amount
Current condition:
0.2% (defect rate)

Prepared by:
Rotary Drive Dept.
Machinery Section
Date:

Theme: Zero Crank Pin Offset Defects

Part	Check Items (for condition control)	Condition Settings — Standard Values	Condition Settings — Quality Impact	Measurement Method (must be illustrated)	Survey Results — Measured Values	Survey Results — Quality Impact	Survey Results — Evaluation	Improvements	Results
Chuck body	• Fastening torque	180 kg/cm	Yes	Torque wrench	100 kg/cm	Yes	X	Install a torque wrench	O
	• Perpendicular to inner diameter	5 µm total length	Yes	Angle gauge	2 µm	None	O		
	• Collet retainer fastened correctly? (In-row section backdash?)	0	Yes	Dial gauge	0	None	O		
Pusher	• Position adjustment error after pusher changeover	Right-left: 0.1 - .5 mm	Yes	Gap gauge	0	Yes	X		
		Up-down: 0.1 - .5 mm	Yes	Gap gauge	0.2 mm	None	O	Readjust using gap gauge	0.2mm
Workpiece holder	• Loose bolt(s)	None allowed	Yes	Hex wrench	0.05 mm	None	O		
	• Pusher moves at an angle	0 – 0.1 mm	Yes	Dial gauge	0.6 mm	None	O		
	• Adjustment error after pin alignment	Right-left: 0.1 - .5 mm	Yes	Gap gauge	0.2 mm	Yes	X	Readjust using gap gauge	0.2mm
		Up-down: 0.1 - .5 mm	Yes	Gap gauge		None	O		
Collet retainer	• Loose bolt(s)	None allowed	Yes	Hex wrench		None	O	Replace	O
Collet	• Edge wear in tapered section	5 µm	Yes		17 µm	Yes	X	Replace	O
	• Edge wear in tapered section	Front: 5 µm Back: 9 µm	Yes	Roundness measurement device	Front: 7 µm Back: 3 µm	Yes	X	Replace	O
	• Edge wear in small diameter section	5 µm	Yes	Roundness measurement device	6 mm	Yes	X	Replace	O

Part	Check Items (for condition control)	Condition Settings		Measurement Method (must be illustrated)	Survey Results		Evaluation	Improvements	Results
		Standard Values	Quality Impact		Measured Values	Quality Impact			
Thrust sleeve	Edge wear in tapered section	9 μm	Yes	Roundness measurement device	5 μm	None	O		
	Debris caught between collet and collet retainer	None allowed	Yes	Visual inspection		Packing stuck in collet in two places	X	Clean out	O
	Debris caught between collet and thrust sleeve	None allowed	Yes	Visual inspection		Fine grinding swarf caught	X	Clean out	O
	Debris caught between workpiece and collet	None allowed	Yes	Visual inspection		Fine grinding swarf caught	X	Clean out	O
	Backlash in chuck body and thrust sleeve	13 – 18 μm	Yes	Micrometer	15 μm		O		
	Space attachment side perpendicular to chuck body guide	5 μm	Yes	Dial gauge	5 μm	None	O		
Positioning guide plate	Block gauge attachment side perpendicular to positioning guide plate	5 μm	Yes	Dial gauge	23 μm	Yes	X	Correct to 5 microns at grinding process	O
Block gauge	Fastening torque	180 kg/cm	Yes	Torque wrench	80 kg/cm	Yes	X	Install torque wrench	O
	Variation in thickness?	2 μm	Yes	Micrometer	2 μm	None	O		
	Flatness	1 μm	Yes	Electric micrometer	1 μm	None	O		
	Is the dimension correct when both block gauge and thickness gauge are used?	2 μm	Yes	Micrometer	8 μm	Yes	X	Make a block gauge to avoid having to use a thickness gauge	O

TABLE 7-16 : REVIEW OF SURVEY RESULTS (CONTINUED)

Part	Check Items (for condition control)	Condition Settings			Survey Results				Improvements	Results
		Standard Values	Quality Impact	Measurement Method (must be illustrated)	Measured Values	Quality Impact	Evaluation			
	Is the gap between the thrust sleeve and the main spindle's gray section correct?	No side contact or pinching allowed	Yes	Dial gauge	0	None	○			
	Workpiece inserted at an angle		Yes	Visual Inspection		Due to setup error, the workpiece was inserted with the rear face at an angle	X	Improve workpiece insertion plate	○
Bearing section	Front: Up-down backlash	2 μm or less	Yes	Dial gauge	2 μm	None	○		
	Right-left backlash	2 μm or less	Yes	Dial gauge	2 μm	None	○		
	Rear Section: Up-down backlash	2 μm or less	Yes	Dial gauge	2 μm	None	○		
	Right-left backlash	2 μm or less	Yes	Dial gauge	2 μm	None	○		
	Debris caught in bearing	Not enough forced air?	Yes	Visual inspection		None	○		

TABLE 7-17: IMPROVEMENT EXAMPLES

	Workpiece-related	Workpiece-related	Operation-related
Survey Item	Block gauge fastening torque	Contact with workpiece holder	Workpiece insertion angle
Standard Value	Fastening torque: 180 kg/cm	Gap width: 0.1 to 0.5	None allowed
Survey Findings	Fastening torque had been determined by operators' subjective judgments (variation in fastening torque caused dimensional variation during changeover)	Zero gap on one side (dimensional variation due to pinching of collet during chucking)	Collet section pinched due to setup error
Improvement	(Use torque wrench)	Collet / Workpiece holder / Before Improvement / Workpiece holder / After Improvement	Before Improvement / Workpiece insertion stand / Workpiece insertion stand / Inserted at an angle / After Improvement / Open gap
Results	**Fastening torque maintained as constant**	**No more pinching during chucking**	**Now inserting workpiece straight, with no more pinching**

TABLE 7-18: CHANGEOVER INSTRUCTIONS FOR RC SMALL PIN GRINDER

Step	Description	Tools	Caution Points
1. Stop grindstone	Push-button operation		Confirm that grindstone has stopped
2. Set auto mode	Change select switch from auto to manual		
3. Raise grindstone cover	Change select switch from middle position to high position		
4. Emergency stop	Push-button operation		
5. Replace offset block gauge	(1) Loosen four M8 bolts in chuck body 	Use custom-made 6 mm hex wrench 	Loosen by only one turn
	(2) Loosen thrust sleeve stabilizing bolt (M8 bolt) 	Use custom-made 6 mm hex wrench 	Loosen by only one turn
	(3) Release latch and give the main spindle one half turn	By hand	
	(4) Loosen block gauge stabilizing bolt (M10 bolt) 	Use custom-made 8 mm hex wrench 	Loosen only until the block gauge can be removed
	(5) Remove block gauge		
	(6) Clean up-down guide	Cleaning cloth	Make sure the guide is thoroughly cleaned (no debris remaining), from the chuck body (bottom) to the positioning guide plate (top)
	(7) Attach a specified replacement block gauge		Make sure the block gauge is thoroughly cleaned (no debris remaining)
	(8) Lightly tighten the block gauge stabilizing bolt (M10 bolt)	Use custom-made 8 mm hex wrench	Pull up chuck body until it reaches the positioning guide plate
	(9) Give the main spindle a half turn to return it to its original position	By hand	
	(10) Tighten the chuck body's four M8 bolts to a torque strength of 30 kg/cm	Use a torque wrench and the custom-made 6 mm hex wrench 	
	(11) Release the latch and give the main spindle a half turn	By hand	**Be absolutely sure you have followed this sequence and have applied the specified torques**
	(12) Tighten the block gauge's stabilizing bolt (M10 bolt) to a torque of 180 kg/cm	Use a torque wrench and the custom-made hex wrench	
	(13) Give the main spindle a half turn to return it to its original position	By hand	
	(14) Tighten the chuck body M8 bolts to a torque of 180 kg/cm	Use a torque wrench and the custom-made hex wrench	
	(15) Tighten the thrust sleeve's stabilizing bolt (M8 bolt)	Use the custom-made hex wrench	

Results

As shown in Figure 7-33, the end result of all these improvements was zero offset defects—the team's original target. In fact, they can now maintain defect-free operation from the time immediately after each changeover. The variation in quality is so small that adjustments are no longer necessary (Figure 7-34). Adjustment procedures that once required experienced operators were eliminated; temporary employees can now set up and run the production equipment without errors. All told, these improvements have reduced cost in employee-hour requirements as well as cost of quality.

Preventive Measures

To maintain the defect-free conditions established, the team devised and used a quality maintenance matrix (Figure 7-35) based on P-M analyses conducted for different defect modes. Along with this matrix, team members also maintained a troubleshooting guide (Table 7-19) for abnormalities discovered in routine maintenance.

FIGURE 7-33: OFFSET DEFECT TRENDS

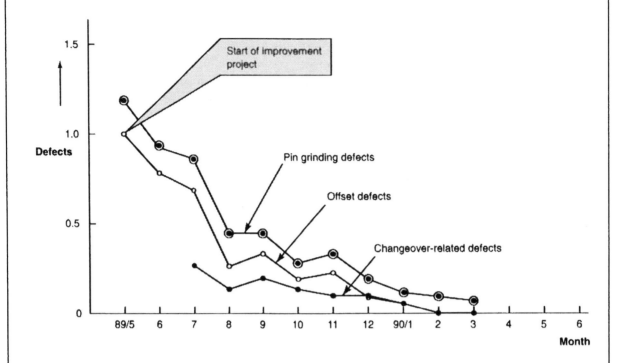

FIGURE 7-34: CRANK OFFSET MEASUREMENTS

Measurement date: December 12, 1989
Measurement start time: 10:30 AM

After Improvement
(after P-M analysis)

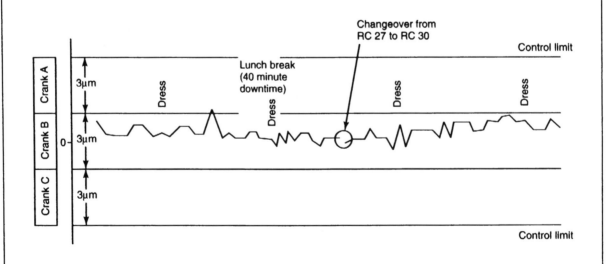

FIGURE 7-35: QUALITY MAINTENANCE MATRIX

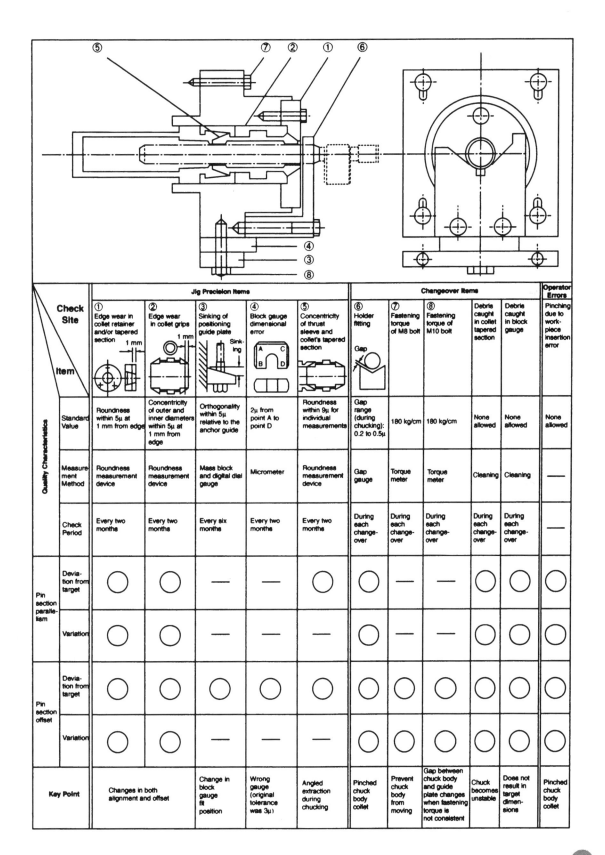

Check Site / Item	Jig Precision Items ① Edge wear in collet retainer and/or tapered section	② Edge wear in collet grips	③ Sinking of positioning guide plate	④ Block gauge dimensional error	⑤ Concentricity of thrust sleeve and collet's tapered section	Changeover Items ⑥ Holder fitting (Gap)	⑦ Fastening torque of M8 bolt	⑧ Fastening torque of M10 bolt	Debris caught in collet tapered section	Debris caught in block gauge	Operator Errors Pinching due to workpiece insertion error
Standard Value	Roundness within 5μ at 1 mm from edge	Concentricity of outer and inner diameters within 5μ at 1 mm from edge	Orthogonality within 5μ relative to the anchor guide	2μ from point A to point D	Roundness within 9μ for individual measurements	Gap range (during chucking): 0.2 to 0.5μ	180 kg/cm	180 kg/cm	None allowed	None allowed	None allowed
Measurement Method	Roundness measurement device	Roundness measurement device	Mass block and digital dial gauge	Micrometer	Roundness measurement device	Gap gauge	Torque meter	Torque meter	Cleaning	Cleaning	—
Check Period	Every two months	Every two months	Every six months	Every two months	Every two months	During each changeover	During each changeover	During each changeover	During each changeover	During each changeover	—
Pin section parallelism — Deviation from target	○	○	—	—	○	○	—	—	○	○	○
Pin section parallelism — Variation	○	○	—	—	—	○	—	—	○	○	○
Pin section offset — Deviation from target	○	○	○	○	○	○	○	○	○	○	○
Pin section offset — Variation	○	○	—	—	—	○	○	○	○	○	○
Key Point	Changes in both alignment and offset		Change in block gauge fit position	Wrong gauge (original tolerance was 3μ)	Angled extraction during chucking	Pinched chuck body collet	Prevent chuck body from moving	Gap between chuck body and guide plate changes when fastening torque is not consistent	Chuck becomes unstable	Does not result in target dimensions	Pinched chuck body collet

TABLE 7-19: TROUBLESHOOTING GUIDE FOR CRANK PIN GRINDING OFFSET DEFECTS

Conditions During Changeover	Causes		Countermeasures
• Parallelism OK but at a larger dimension than target dimension	1. Wrong block gauge dimensions	• Wrong gauge	• Replace gauge
	2. Insufficient block gauge fastening strength	• Fastening torque of M10 bolt is less than standard value	• If 180 kg/cm is not enough, raise torque to 200 kg/cm
		• Insufficient nut and bolt strength	• Replace and then retighten (for practice)
	3. Debris and burrs caught in block gauge	• Debris and/or burrs caught between the gauge contact side and the jig or positioning guide plate	• Clean and then reset
• Parallelism OK but at a smaller dimension than target	1. Wrong block gauge dimensions	• Wrong gauge rank • Wear on gauge	• Replace gauge • After measuring dimensions, replace if more than 2 microns over table value
	2. Positioning guide plate is defective	• Wear on gauge contact side • Gauge contact side has sunk	• Replace • After grinding for orthogonality, repair to within 5 microns
	3. Poor fit of chuck body with gauge contact side	• Wear on gauge contact side	• Replace body
• Dimension larger than target with high parallelism on rear shaft side High	1. Edge wear on retainer and collet	• Wear on retainer and collet tapered section	• Replace retainer if roundness is not within 5μm • Replace collet if roundness is not within 5μm
	2. Debris caught in retainer and collet tapered section	• Debris caught in retainer and collet lower section	• Must be cleaned
January 13, 1990	Daikin Kōgyō		

About the Authors

Kunio Shirose is executive vice president of JIPM, senior consultant, and director of TPM General Research Institute. Mr. Shirose was a consultant with the Japan Management Association for 24 years before joining JIPM in 1984 to specialize in TPM. He has worked with many companies, including Fujikoshi, Nissan, Dai Nippon Printing, Nippon Electric, and Daikin. He is co-author of *TPM Development Program,* author of *TPM for Workshop Leaders,* and advisory editor of *TPM for Operators* (English editions published by Productivity Press).

Yoshifumi Kimura is TPM consultant with JIPM and TPM General Research Institute. After helping develop TPM at Nachi-Fujikoshi, Mr. Kimura joined JIPM as a consultant and has worked with Konica, Daikin, Fuji Industries, and other companies. He co-authored *Training for TPM* (Productivity Press) and also wrote a book on equipment management for operators (published in Japanese). He also made several excellent presentations at the first TPM conference in 1990.

Mitsugu Kaneda is TPM consultant with JIPM and TPM General Research Institute. He was instrumental in implementing TPM at Nachi-Fujikoshi and was the director of the company's TPM promotion office. Mr. Kaneda joined JIPM in 1994 and has worked with Matsushita Electric, Sanyo Electric, Tokyo Sekisui, and other companies for TPM implementation. Mr. Kaneda is co-author of *Training for TPM* (Productivity Press) and a book on equipment improvement activity for operators (published in Japanese).

Index

Printed in the United States
33804LVS00003B/67-100

9 781563 273124

Made in the USA
Lexington, KY
21 June 2016